PRAISE FOR
IN/ACTION—RETHINKING THE PATH TO RESULTS

"These days, we are all too busy, pushing forward and driving results. But Jinny Uppal provides a fresh perspective: in some cases, taking action might not be the solution, but the *problem*. Read this book to discover an empowering framework to help you make smart decisions and get the best results."

—Dorie Clark, Global Thinker in Thinkers 50,
WSJ Best-Selling Author, *The Long Game*

"Passionate. An inspired call that melds history, biography, and social science together to foster how we might better approach action within ourselves and others."

—Eugene Soltes, Professor at Harvard Business School,
Author, *Why They Do It: Inside the Mind
of the White-Collar Criminal*

"As a corporate leader at multiple Fortune 100 companies, this book gave me pause to reconsider my own action bias and that there are multiple paths to desired outcomes. I will be recommending IN/ACTION to all my friends and colleagues."

—Julie Elmore, Chief Technology Officer, Dollar General
Corporation

"What if all the business gurus advocating a "bias for action" were wrong? Jinny Uppal shows why at times inaction can be the best strategy. She backs up this counterintuitive concept with stories and research that demonstrate how doing nothing, or at least pausing, often leads to better outcomes. Uppal teaches you a new way to think about making decisions, handling crises, and even responding to personal attacks. One action you shouldn't delay: reading *IN/ACTION!*"

—Roger Dooley, International Keynote Speaker
and Author of *Friction and Brainfluence*

"An absorbing collection of stories and research woven through crisp leadership takeaways, *IN/ACTION* illustrates how thoughtful, intentional pauses can empower incredible success."

—Lindsay Kaplan, Founder of Chief,
Senior Women's Executive Network

"In a world that has become blindly focused on hustle culture, Jinny Uppal's book is a breath of fresh air that reminds us to pause and reflect on alternative, more efficient paths to desired results in business, nonprofits and life."

—Dan Driscoll, Social Entrepreneur, Ashoka Fellow

"Every overachiever who grew up being taught that we must constantly produce or perform to be successful should read this book. Jinny Uppal presents a much-needed alternative which helps us accomplish more and often better by doing less. This book digs deep into the stories of successful people from multiple walks of life and truly illustrates the power of strategic inaction, when much of life's magic takes place, leading to great results and overall well-being.

—Pavita Singh, Mental Health Advocate,
Author, *To All The Magic In Me*

IN/ACTION

Dearest Usha

Thank you for your support
Hope this book helps open
up new paths to success

IN/ACTION

RETHINKING THE PATH TO RESULTS

JINNY UPPAL

NEW DEGREE PRESS

IN/ACTION
Rethinking the Path to Results

ISBN   978-1-63730-902-5 *Paperback*
            978-1-63730-750-2 *Kindle Ebook*
            978-1-63730-996-4 *Ebook*

To my parents, whom I lost too young, too soon.

It was late summer in 1999; I was getting ready to move from grad school in Miami to New Jersey to start my first-ever job. I was excited and nervous. I called to update my parents in Bombay on all my plans: the new job, the new town, the apartment I had rented, the used car I had bought. The next time I called, Mom said, "Your dad has been calling all the relatives to ask them how they are doing." That was odd, I thought. Dad never made social calls; that was Mom's department. "He then gets to the point," she continued. "'Mini called from America,' he says, (referring to me by my nickname). 'She bought a BMW.'"

I picture the two of them sitting up in heaven now. They have finished reading my letter. Dad is sitting cross-legged, as always. Mom is next to him with her phone book open, telling him who to call next. "Mini wrote from Earth," says my dad to the people he calls. "She published her book."

TABLE OF CONTENTS

———

कर्मण्यकर्म य: परयेदकर्मणि च कर्म य:
स बुद्धिमान्मनुष्येषु स युक्त: कृत्स्नकर्मकृत्

karmaṇyakarma yaḥ paśhyed akarmaṇi
ćha karma yaḥ sa buddhimān manuṣhyeṣhu
sa yuktaḥ kṛitsna-karma-kṛit

Those who see action in inaction and
inaction in action are truly wise amongst humans.
Although performing all kinds of actions, they are
yogis and masters of all their actions.

Bhagavad Gita, Chapter 4, Verse 18

INTRODUCTION

"The skillful leader subdues the enemy without any fighting, he captures their cities without laying siege to them, he overthrows their kingdom without lengthy operations in the field. With his forces intact, he will dispute the mastery of the Empire, thus, without losing a man, his triumph will be complete. This is the method of attacking by stratagem."

—SUN TZU, *THE ART OF WAR*

It's 1812, and Napoleon is headed your way with over one hundred thousand soldiers, his Grand Armée. You are a Russian general, Mikhail Kutuzov, an old, battle-worn, wizened soldier and general, holding firm in Moscow. Napoleon's planned attack on Moscow is the highest form of aggression. It is, in fact, an attack on all of Russia.

Fully dressed in your soldier's uniform and battle ready, you stand over a mass of maps, pouring over them, while surrounded by your staff and comrades. You all review Napoleon's path and how long it will take for him to get to Moscow. Your lieutenants make recommendations on where and how you should counterattack. The boss man, Czar Alexander, expects to hear of your plans to attack and arrest Napoleon's progress.

Your entire military career has centered on taking decisive action. The enemy approaches. The threat is clear and visible. You need to take action before he gets to Moscow. You need to stop him.

What *do* you do? Do you attack him on his way? Or do you get ready to defend?

General Kutuzov chooses neither.

He chooses to retreat. He evacuates and abandons Moscow. His comrades keep urging him to take action, but he chooses to wait. He says to himself over and over, like a mantra: *Time and patience. Patience and time*

Napoleon marches on. His plan was to take over Moscow. And he does just that. He now expects a formal surrender.

But no one is there to surrender. Everyone is gone. The troops are gone. The residents are gone too. On the way out, the army and civilians have set the city on fire.

Here is Napoleon, in an abandoned city with no food for his troops, helplessly watching the fires burn everything in sight. It's October—it's cold in Moscow, with subzero temperatures. He knows he needs to head back, or his troops will not survive the winter without food and supplies. He orders his troops to start for France. But he has underestimated the harsh conditions of the Russian countryside. Hypothermia sets in for many of his soldiers and horses. His army is decimated. Napoleon makes it back to France but with only a fraction of his Grand Armée.

According to Jesse Greenspan in his historical analysis, this defeat was the beginning of the end for Napoleon.

Kutuzov wasn't paralyzed into inaction because of fear. His apparent inaction was a thoughtful choice to not default to a counterattack or defense. He achieved his goal of defeating Napoleon. You might say he exceeded his goal by dealing a crushing defeat without expending the usual cost of delivering such a defeat: lives of soldiers.

TO ACT OR NOT TO ACT

We tend to celebrate action, especially acts of heroism and bravado. Most success stories are associated with what the protagonist *did*. Kutuzov didn't win any kudos for retreating and letting time and weather take its toll. Stories of pausing, patience, or waiting aren't glamorous or heroic to tell.

Why is that? Why don't we celebrate the pause? The strategic waiting. The off-playbook but thoughtful inaction. Is it because that approach usually doesn't lead to a win? I wondered if Kutuzov's was a one-off fortuitous story or an approach that could be studied and repeated.

What I found has changed the way I see ambition, action, results, and the relationship between them.

The definition of ambition is closely linked with a desire for success and power. And yet, the more ambitious we are, the more likely we are to struggle with stress and anxiety. A 2014 research study conducted at the University of California, Berkeley, found a "strong correlation between the highs and lows of perceived power and mood disorders," especially among the young. The world has become more competitive. There are more options to choose from; more information comes at us than ever before. Technology has disrupted every part of our lives, in both good and destructive ways. Newer ways of working and newer opportunities pop up everywhere and every day. Fifty years ago, the world had less of everything to choose from: fewer professions, career paths, and even dating platforms (you met your sweetheart through family, college, or work, instead of swiping right on dozens of dating apps in existence today). Now there is more of everything to choose from. Even the choice of college majors has grown in the United States. There are thirty more majors today compared to fifty years ago.

All this advancement has a downside. The more information that we are taking in, which needs to be processed, the more overwhelming the task of making a choice has become. We think we need to work hard to achieve our goals. But no matter what choices we make, there's always a feeling of uncertainty. Maybe we should be doing more or working harder. The more there is to choose from and to achieve, the more action we take toward our goals.

In chasing our goals, we start chasing action.

In our lives, hard work translates into a lot of doing. Action requires expenditure of resources, both mental and physical. Doing takes effort, which in turn consumes energy. Most productivity hacks are about doing more. Unfortunately, time doesn't expand; only the list of to-dos does. To compensate, we give up on rest and load up on stimulants, like coffee or prescription drugs, further compromising our energy levels. According to a *Forbes* article, people between twenty and thirty-nine are the fastest growing population segment for stimulant prescriptions.

Hard work then translates into long working hours, which lead to poor health. A 2021 global study from the World Health Organization found that working fifty-five hours or more a week was linked to a 35 percent higher risk of stroke and a 17 percent higher risk of dying from ischemic heart disease, compared to a thirty-five-to-forty-hour work week. This study included data from over 154 countries across multiple lines of work and measured the impact of long hours over several years.

FROM LONG HOURS TO HEALTH BREAKDOWN

Chasing action is not sustainable in the short term either. No matter how much we employ productivity tips to cram more into the day, there's always a feeling of falling behind. We never have enough hours in the day. In our single-minded pursuit of our goals, we ignore aspects of life such as health and well-being. When we are young, we think we will have time to attend to that later. Before we know it, this habit of chasing action turns into a behavioral trait that stays with us as we age. For many, a wake-up call comes in the form of burnout, sickness, or estrangement from family and loved ones. Often, in our determined pursuit of results, we choose the wrong actions that either push the result away or create another set of problems. Chasing action can lead to avoidable mistakes. I have made a few mistakes myself, which I will share in later chapters.

It doesn't have to be that way.

Ambition is something to be celebrated. There's nothing wrong in wanting results or success. A desire for success is an innate part of who we are. It's what drives progress. I believe we can achieve desired results without paying the price of chasing action. In my interviews and research, I found it is possible to avoid unnecessary or counterproductive action. In looking back into my own life, I have deployed this approach with better-than-expected results.

I moved to the United States from Mumbai, India, for grad school in my early twenties, highly unusual for unmarried females with my cultural background. I pivoted twice in my career, moved cross country and back while working at companies ranging from $250 million to $19 billion dollars in sales, growing to become vice president of strategy for a $12 billion–dollar North American retail business. Somewhere in that journey, I took a sabbatical to work with artisans in Morocco. I noticed that every one of my big and bold moves was preceded by a phase during which I felt underproductive, even lazy. I hated those phases. Looking back, it was in the middle of apparent inaction that the seeds of the next big idea were being sown. A kind of momentum was building up during these outwardly inactive phases. And when I felt ready, I made my move. More recently, this book was borne out of my boredom and restlessness during the inactivity imposed on us all during the 2020 pandemic.

What has changed after writing this book is that instead of hating the periods I would have described as wastefully underproductive, I better appreciate the power of what looks like inactivity but isn't.

As part of my book research, I interviewed over thirty people across Europe, North America, and India—each considered successful in their sphere of life. What I have discovered from these interviews, my own life experiences, and from established research studies is this: While chasing action can very well lead to results, it takes *mastering action* to achieve remarkable results. And the fastest way to mastering action is by leveraging *strategic inaction.*

Action uses up time, mental and physical energy, and other personal resources. While some action is required to get to results, there is almost always a less expensive way (by taking less action) to getting those results.

Mastering action is knowing when to act and when not to act. Strategic, or thoughtful, inaction is a lever that leads to results with less expenditure of resources.

Think back to Kutuzov. By retreating, he conserved his main resource: the lives of his soldiers. He didn't officially surrender even after Napoleon took over Moscow. He did nothing but wait for Napoleon to decide on his next course of action, which was to head back to France. Kutuzov leveraged strategic inaction.

While Napoleon was on his way back, Kutuzov finally acted. He strategically attacked Napoleon, forcing his army on a route that increased the probability of starvation. By choosing to retreat at first, Kutuzov built up momentum: His army was rested and strong; the opponent's was fatigued and weak. He let the unexpectedly brutal winter cause damage to his opponent's army. When he did take action, he weakened Napoleon's army enough to make sure they wouldn't rebuild or return.

By conserving energy you would have spent on chasing action, you leave your mind open to discovering off-playbook and nonlinear paths to results. You allow unexpected and serendipitous events to reveal opportunities to you. You build up momentum and then deploy resources to maximum advantage when the circumstances are right.

PARALIZING VS STRATEGIC INACTION

Strategic, or thoughtful, inaction is different from inaction that comes from fear or inertia. That would be inaction caused by helplessness and mental paralysis. Strategic inaction is a choice; it requires original thinking. It is not "letting the chips fall where they may." It is awareness that the default action is not the right choice in that moment and that inaction is the better option.

It is a period of pause to allow for inspired action to show up.

ABOUT THIS BOOK

This book is not about pausing for the sake of it or about slowing down as an end goal. In fact, this book is about developing a path to results and success—without paying the typical price of nonstop doing.

Platitudes such as "money/success aren't everything" aside, we are always working toward something: a job, a life partner, buying a home, a startup exit, a nonprofit launch. Contrary to the usual action-packed formulaic advice such as "ten things you need to do to [fill in your goal]," this book is about *leveraging the power of strategic inaction to find a nonlinear path to great results.*

Kutuzov is one example; we will visit other stories of strategic inaction. What if we don't do what the experts, wisdom of the masses, or our own mind compel us to do? What if we are like Singh, CEO of a major global medical imaging firm, who was informed of the death of a child on a machine made by his company and went for a two-hour walk instead of immediately calling an emergency staff meeting and lawyering up? What if we, like Tyler Hayes, a successful Silicon Valley founder, shunned the proven venture capital route for fundraising and chose the far easier and less stressful (and less used) crowd-funding path for our fourth business? Spoiler alert: They both got far better results and unexpected wins.

This book explores stories of those who have "made it" by usual social standards: success, wealth, overall life satisfaction. It explores the approaches and mental models they used. It looks into research on the science of inactivity and doing nothing. Lastly, it provides an approach to developing mastery of action through strategic inaction. Ultimately, this book is about making room for inspired action to lead us on a nonlinear path to great results.

In part one, we will explore why and how we got here. We will explore how ambition, aspiration, and even self-awareness create progress, as well as the tendency of chasing action.

Part two is about the major obstacles to mastering action and our tendency to default to a playbook, create narrow and rigid goals, and create cause and effect where none exists.

Part three explores habits we can develop to counter our action bias. We will discover how daydreaming, mind-wandering, laziness, and procrastination—usually scorned behaviors—can provide access to creative ideas and inspired action.

Chapters in parts one through three have questions at the end that are meant to be contemplated. I recommend chewing them over; don't be in a hurry to answer them.

While action and inaction may seem like black-and-white choices, in part four we will discover a perspective on mastery of action that requires going beyond this apparent dichotomy. The last chapter has a summary of takeaways from the book.

By the time you are finished reading, I will have demonstrated and hopefully convinced you of this:

FROM RUNNING THE HAMSTER WHEEL
TO SURFING THE WAVE OF LIFE

Life is not as hard as it seems. Life is not a hamster wheel, which runs only if we keep running. Something much more than our actions makes our world go around. It is worth stopping long enough to connect with the undulating flow of life. It is worth riding this flow of life, which can carry us further than we could ever go with our own doing alone.

PART 1

HOW WE
GOT HERE

CHAPTER 1

AMBITION AND
THE ACTION BIAS

———

"To do nothing is often the best course of action. But history was not made by those who did nothing. So I suppose it's only natural that ambitious and driven men want to go down in history."

—QUEEN ELIZABETH II'S COMMENTS ON PRIME
MINISTER EDEN'S ACTIONS AS DEPICTED IN THE
NETFLIX SHOW *THE CROWN*, SEASON 2

The Suez Canal Crisis began on October 29, 1956, when Egyptian president Gamal Abdel Nasser nationalized the canal, a valuable waterway that controlled two-thirds of the oil used by Europe. Anthony Eden had become prime minister of the United Kingdom the prior year. Vowing to reclaim the "great imperial lifeline," he decided to take action. He orchestrated a covert agreement with Israel and France to launch an attack on Egypt. This agreement came to light soon after the three countries attacked, seemingly independently. In a rare show of unity, the United States and Russia condemned this overt act of aggression and demanded an immediate withdrawal, which the three countries had no choice but to follow.

Some historians believe all that actioning was Eden's way of demonstrating his power and leadership as prime minister. Unfortunately, he was forced to undo his action, causing enough humiliation that he had to resign, ending his short-lived time as prime minister. Unlike Kutuzov in the previous chapter, Eden couldn't wait to take action. His misguided urgency to act cost him his job, not to mention risking international relations.

This episode in history was depicted in the 2016 Netflix show *The Crown*. Queen Elizabeth's quote above, lamenting the tendency of people wanting to act even when doing nothing is the best choice, isn't limited to ambitious prime ministers.

Humans are wired to acknowledge and celebrate action far more than inaction. Action can be perceived and discussed in a tangible form. It's easy to see the effects of our action and effort. Inaction is harder to acknowledge and appreciate. It's hard to demonstrate causality between what we didn't do and positive outcomes. On the flip side, it's easier to see the causality between what we don't do and a negative outcome. Our ancestors foraged for food. If they didn't take the action of foraging, they didn't eat. When farming was introduced and we domesticated animals, we had a lot more to do with the land and farm animals. We introduced automations such as a yoke and other early technologies to make life easier. We associated all that *doing* with progress. Instead, life kept getting more complex, and we kept adding even more to-dos until it became a trap. The only way to get out of that trap was waiting until the next generation took over, retirement, or death.

In modern times, we have gone beyond our need to survive. We now pursue success, accomplishment, power. We are commended from our childhood for what we did, achieved, or accomplished. We, especially male children, start idolizing action figures of young heroes and heroines who do brave and bold things to save the world. The phrase "action figure" itself came into being in 1964 when toy maker Hasbro launched their new G.I. Joe, a toy soldier targeting boys. They didn't think "doll for boys" was going to sell, hence the more exciting phrase. As per *Merriam-Webster*, the meaning of the word "power" is inextricably linked with action.

All these words capture our imagination and give rise to our earliest aspirations. They teach us that doing and exerting ourselves is the right way of being successful and worthy. In turn, this creates an illusion of control over outcomes through our actions. The greater our ambition is, the more we want to control outcomes.

The pursuit of success is ironic. In our youth, in life, and in work, we train ourselves to work hard and put in effort toward our goals. If we are not successful in getting results, the more ambitious and intrepid among us double down on our "efforting." Say we succeed. We get the wonderful spouse, family, job, or business we always wanted. That creates another problem. Those around us—families, employees, teammates—start expecting us to do more. The higher up the ladder of life we go, the more people around us expect that we are the ones to make things happen. In addition to all the pressure we put on ourselves, we are now faced with compounding pressure from others to act. But the fact is that the more complex our life and work is, the less we control outcomes with direct action.

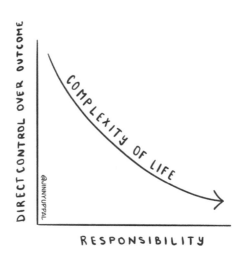

In 2012, I joined Kohl's, a large retailer in the United States, to help drive their business transformation. Then-CEO Kevin Mansell had embarked on an ambitious plan to transform the company inside out in the next few years. As he unveiled his grand plan of driving business growth—fittingly called "The Greatness Agenda"—to the leaders of the company, he said something about power and control at top levels that left a deep impression on my mind. He started off by sharing that people often think CEOs have the power to make things happen.

Paraphrasing, he said, "I wish I could tell you how different things look from my point of view. From where I am standing, *you* have the power. You, who owns specific functions, can do something about it. I can only share my vision and try to influence you." He shared that when he was a merchant, in a junior role, he had control over specific aspects of the business. As he climbed up the ladder, the ability to control outcomes through his actions reduced. His body language, more than his words, communicated an authentic helplessness and a plea to his audience that without their participation and action, "The Greatness Agenda" was doomed.

As Mansell went on to lead his company through a successful transformation, his final act of non-doing was executing his own succession. When he retired in 2018, he replaced himself with someone he had previously hired. As of this writing, Kohl's continues to be more successful than many of its peers in an otherwise struggling retail industry.

You don't have to be a CEO to be higher up in life. Do you have a team you work with? Do you have children? Are you married? Are you a student enrolled in classes while doing volunteer work? Do you have a side hustle and hobbies? Then your life is complex enough. You have enough responsibilities to know or to find out you can't control everything around you with your actions.

Even though we celebrate qualities such as action orientation, determination, and decisiveness, I have come to learn, from my own personal experience, that the same qualities can get in the way of the very goals we are trying to achieve.

JUMPING FROM THE FRYING PLAN INTO THE FIRE

It was like any other summer day. I had come back home from office to find the red button blinking on my voicemail machine. This was 2000, back in the day when we had landlines with an attached recording machine that stored voicemails. On this day, like any other, I pushed the button. It was a short, terse message from my brother in Mumbai.

"Mini," it started, addressing me by my nickname. "Mom is no more. She is no more Mini. Call me."

I sat down on my bed next to the phone. Thoughts raced through my mind: *How could this be! I was in Mumbai just three weeks ago. We had celebrated my birthday. She was fine.* My mom had a heart attack ten years before this and an angioplasty after that. We had no indication her heart was in trouble again. *She looked fine when I saw her. How was this possible?* And yet, there was no mistaking what my brother had said. A short conversation with him told me the rest: It all happened suddenly, and she died of a cardiac arrest before reaching the hospital.

This is not how it was supposed to turn out. I am the youngest of five, a fourth daughter, raised in a middle-class family in Mumbai, the biggest city of India, during the 1980s and '90s. Life in our circle was fairly predictable. If you were a boy, you got married at around twenty-three years of age and joined your father's business. If you were a girl, you got married at twenty-two and became a homemaker. Some girls went to college, but it was a matter of passing the time while waiting to get married. Your parents would find a suitable mate for you. My parents were the exception. Rather, my mother was. Knowing she would never raise enough dowry for four daughters, she was clear that she would get us a higher education so we could "make [our] own money and not depend on anyone else." And so, three years before this event, I had traveled to the United States for grad school. The plan was to graduate, get a year of work experience, move back to India, get a job, get married, and blend into the rhythm of normal life.

And now this. In those few seconds, sitting at the edge of my bed, thoughts continued racing at top speed. *All my older siblings are married, with children, complete with families of their own.* While my father was still alive, the gender roles of those times were such that my mother would have been the one to watch out for my social future. She would have ensured I got married, which was the next step in the plan. *Now, I am on my own. I need to take care of myself.*

By early 2001, I got more bad news. My father had been diagnosed with Hepatitis C. The doctors had given him two years to live. I decided to take matters into my own hands and fill this fast-widening hole in my family life. I decided I would get married. I started dating Greg, whom I had met at work. Every few weeks, I got an update from home, with a reduced life expectancy for my dad. In equal measure, my commitment to Greg went up. He had his own reasons to get married soon. He was turning thirty, which was late in his Armenian circles. We set a date for October.

One weekend in July that year, I got a call from my brother. Our father would not make it through the weekend. During that time, Greg was away with poor cellphone reception, and

I couldn't reach him. I couldn't speak to my father either. By the end of the weekend, one year and one month after my mother's passing, my father died. The voice in my head grew more urgent: *I have been left behind; I have been abandoned.* Normally, when a family member dies, the tradition in our family is to postpone celebrations for a year, especially weddings. I, on the other hand, made another decision to act. I would marry right away. I insisted I did not want to wait. Everyone agreed with the plan. My siblings were distraught with the rapid turn of events and seemed to trust my decisiveness. Greg agreed. And so, less than six months from our first date and a week after my father's death, we were married.

Almost immediately, I knew I had made a massive mistake. Our temperaments, lifestyle, and value systems were a significant mismatch. What had I done? In my fear and insecurity, I had jumped from the frying pan into the fire. I had no one to blame. This wasn't an arranged marriage. This was on me. My determination combined with a decisiveness had led me to speed up action on a bad decision. Taking the chance to postpone the wedding when my father died would have given me time and space to reconsider. But my action orientation compelled me to act right away.

THE ACTION BIAS

Action bias is a widely researched cognitive behavioral pattern in humans. In their seminal work on the topic, researchers Patt and Zeckhauser define action bias as "a penchant for action…[which] is a product of non-rational behavior." The key part of the definition is that it is a result of "non-rational behavior."

Action bias does not discriminate by age, gender, ethnicity, or social status. Having said that, the more ambitious and determined we are, the more susceptible we are to action bias. It doesn't matter whether our ambition is to end hate crime or to get a promotion; the more goal-oriented we become, the more we are susceptible to irrationally chasing action in order to chase results.

There are three main triggers of action bias that we will address throughout the book:

- Acting without thinking
- Overconfidence
- Regret of loss or potential loss

We will also look into indirect triggers of our action bias: how we set and pursue goals and our tendency to follow a default action playbook and create false causality between our actions and outcomes.

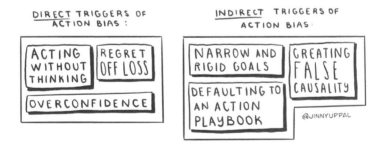

Action bias is not an illness or a disorder; it's a behavioral trait. We are all familiar with some examples of irrational action, for example, reacting to an email when upset.

However, biases have a tendency to operate in our subconscious. More often than not, we are unconsciously operating under the influence of action bias. And like all biases, we can choose to address action bias once we become aware of it and that it doesn't serve us. In the chapters that follow, I will share stories and research on how each of the triggers above can create the tendency to act irrationally and ideas on how to preempt or mitigate that tendency.

CONTEMPLATE
1. Can you think of a time when you jumped into urgent action with undesirable results?
2. Can you think of a time when you didn't jump into the most obvious action path, and it was a hard thing to do (or not do!)?

CHAPTER 2

THE LIGHT AT THE END OF THE ACTION BIAS TUNNEL

———

"I went from wanting to be the guy who responds quickly to the guy who responds responsibly."

—MAHESH KOTHURKAR

Let's take a trip down the darker depths of action bias and then find our way out of it.

The digital revolution combined with the rise of the woke movement have created a side effect in the form of our worsening action bias. Turns out parallels in history will help us understand our current situation better. During my research, I came across American neurologist George Beard's 1881 book entitled *American Nervousness: Its Causes and Consequences.* The book talks about an increase in a new class of functional diseases of the nervous system. Beard writes, "The chief and primary cause of this development and very rapid increase of nervousness is *modern civilization,* which is distinguished from the ancient by these characteristics: steam power, the periodical press, the telegraph, the sciences, the mental activity of women." He coined a term "neurasthenia" to describe a new kind of mental illness due to emotional disturbances and nervousness. This class of diseases "seem to have first taken root under an American sky whence their seed is being distributed [to the rest of the world]."

By the time Beard wrote his book, apart from the technological improvements he mentioned, the country had experienced a variety of social movements and uprisings: the Civil War of the 1860s and the ongoing women's suffrage movement. These movements challenged the norm of white-male dominance, which caused neurasthenia in that society, impacting everyone. Is it not a remarkable coincidence that we are experiencing something similar in the form of digital disruption, social justice, and gender equality movements in the United States? This is in turn causing a ripple effect across the world and acting as a major social stressor for all parties, regardless of gender, race, and ethnicity.

The smartphone and social media are the new steam power, telegraph, and periodical press rolled together and then some. You only have to take one look at reaction-filled social media posts to get a glimpse of how much we have set our teeth on edge as seismic socioeconomic changes occur all around us. Social scientists have called out the influence of social media on rising hate crime across the world, especially toward minorities. As an example, the irrational forwarding of rumors on WhatsApp, a messaging platform, was blamed for the rise in communal violence in India in 2014, according to a Council of Foreign Affairs report.

The rise of technology and the increase in sociocultural tension among religious, ethnic, and racial groups has the effect of worsening our action bias, our tendency to react, sometimes irrationally. Everyone seems to be "acting out."

WHAT HERD ACTING LOOKS LIKE

THE DARK SIDE OF ACTION

In his book on white collar criminals such as Bernie Madoff, *Why They Do It: Inside the Mind of the White-Collar Criminal*, Harvard Business School professor Eugene Soltes interviewed several ambitious and (formerly) powerful and successful men from the corporate and investment world. These men were eventually tried and convicted for white collar fraud. While we may be tempted to attribute such behavior to intrinsic moral or psychological flaws in the perpetrators, Soltes argues that the reasons are far more insidiously simple.

Among them, he attributes the environment the executives operate in, which does not allow for reflective thinking: "The problem is that many executives are constantly engaged in a whirlwind of meetings, travel and emails. With incessant demands on their time, they take few opportunities to slow down, ruminate on their judgments, and engage in this more reflective thinking."

In other words, executives are too busy "doing" to pause on the moral and ethical implications of the myriad of small decisions they make. It starts with small and seemingly harmless actions, like booking a sale just before the quarter ends to meet targets, even though the deal will close a few days after the new quarter begins. And before you know it, a habit of acting unethically builds up in a spiral until it becomes major fraud.

While it's easy to sit in judgment of others who committed fraud, it is worth noting that we are all, at some level, subject to a similar lifestyle of "too busy to even think."

While on the subject of the dark side of action, I connected with Aliza Luft, assistant professor at the University of California Los Angeles's department of sociology. She conducted research on the Rwandan genocide of 1994, where, in a hundred-day period, hundreds of thousands of Tutsis were killed by armed militia along with ordinary Hutu civilians. In her research, Luft interviewed ordinary civilians—not the leaders or masterminds, but those who committed the act of killing.

Luft shared with me, "The people interviewed reported that the more they killed, the easier killing became for them, because they stopped thinking about their murderous actions. Though initially they made choices to kill for various reasons, over time, this active decision-making process faded, and killing became routinized." She concluded that dehumanization in the perpetrators didn't necessarily begin before the genocide. Rather, "it was a consequence of civilians' cognitive adaptation to violence, rendering killing a thoughtless, meaningless act." In other words, they built up a tolerance for large and repetitive harmful actions, killings in this case, over time.

Although white collar crime and genocide may seem far apart on the spectrum of heinous acts, the underlying behavioral traits are the same: a tendency to act without thinking and developing a habit of acting without thinking

All these horrific insights notwithstanding, the takeaway here is that action bias catches us unawares; it starts small and builds up. It follows then that an increase in awareness can help reduce that tendency, as we shall see next.

WHAT WORKED THERE WON'T WORK HERE: UNLEARNING THE ACTION BIAS

Mahesh Kothurkar joined the Indian Navy as a Cadet when he was twenty years old. Ten years into his time in the navy, he was stationed onboard an aircraft carrier and was involved in a fire incident, which was to exacerbate his action bias for years to come.

Kothurkar's role, at the time, was to direct combat drills onboard the carrier, where he guided fighter pilots practicing shooting at the enemy while airborne. Combat drills are physically and emotionally exhausting for everyone involved. After one such intense day, he was sound asleep when the fire alarm broke out. The carrier was old and false alarms had been frequent. Kothurkar woke up groggy, decided to ignore what he assumed was a false alarm and went right back to sleep.

He was shaken awake by a fellow officer telling him there was a fire and he needed to get the hell out of there! Kothurkar rushed up a nearby ladder onto the deck and to safety. Two other officers didn't get out in time and died below deck. All Kothurkar could think was, "I should have gotten out when I first heard the alarm. The officer who wasted precious time waking me up could have saved someone else."

After this incident, he was always "prepared for the worst case." He told me, "The bias for action set in so deeply after this incident that at the slightest sign of trouble, I was ready to take action. I had not taken action that day in the fire, and I regretted that. I lived this way for many years." Living "this way" meant living with constant anxiety and stress: "I was always aware of the possibility of every emergency under my command, I was always prepared. It had an adverse effect on my health." He developed a stress-related chronic illness.

As he got promoted, he became a hands-on leader, always in the middle of the action with his sailors. At the sign of the slightest trouble, he would roll up his sleeves and get down below deck to investigate the issue himself. A typical officer would have stayed on deck and called down orders and questions. His sailors loved his management style.

About twelve years after the fire incident, he retired from the navy as commander and joined a large global conglomerate. A nerve-racking business trip from Johannesburg to Mumbai was to be the scene of a wake-up call. Kothurkar and his manager were to travel together to meet the CEO of the division, a critical meeting for him. Kothurkar, who always prepared for the worst case, suggested they leave four hours early to deal with the bad traffic. While in the chauffeured car, his nervousness got the better of him, and he asked to take over and drive the car. His manager chose this moment to give him feedback that he tended to try too hard to control outcomes. He coached Kothurkar on the need to delegate more often and let the chauffeur take care of the driving.

This was a wake-up call for Kothurkar: "I had to condition myself after this to not be so action oriented." I asked him, "How did you train, or rather 'untrain' yourself?" He described a three-part approach he developed and applied over the years. "One was to condition my mind not to [continuously] talk about 'what if something goes wrong.' If I miss the flight, then I will go back tomorrow. If I miss the meeting with the CEO, it doesn't matter. He will give me another time to meet."

"The second was delegation. I lived by Steven Covey's 'stewardship delegation,'" referring to the Covey's recommendation from his book *Seven Habits of Highly Effective People*. This kind of delegation teaches a manager or leader to describe the desired results and lets their team figure out how they will achieve it, rather than constantly giving them direction on what to do and how to do it.

"The third was to be patient. Sleep over it." In one implementation of this approach, he trained himself to not reply to emails as soon as they arrive. "I went from wanting to be the guy who responds quickly to the guy who responds responsibly."

Regret caused Kothurkar to develop a strong action bias and an always-on leadership style. In the navy, his hands-on nature was appreciated by his staff, even though he paid the price through the effect on his health. But that style didn't work in his corporate job; that very behavior risked getting in the way of effective teamwork. Once he became aware, it was a matter of systematically changing his behavior.

IT'S NEVER TOO LATE TO NOT ACT

Just as Kothurkar had learned a lesson on the downside of his action bias, I had learned mine too. Back to my marriage and the realization that I had made a mistake, an obvious next course of action was divorce. But I wasn't ready to act this time. Part of it was my commitment to my marriage. Part of it was me trying to understand how I got there and what I really wanted next. I had jumped into marriage without thinking what I wanted out of it and life. When I was in India, I wanted independence. Once I got that, I fell into the automatic set of goals I had inherited from the society I grew up in—job, marriage, and so on. It took me four and a half years to become clear on my value system and the life I wanted to live. Back then I wasn't thinking of "inaction as a strategic choice." My saving grace, the reason why it took four plus years, was awareness of my prior hasty action, a lack of clarity on my next steps, and an unwillingness to act without that clarity.

Once I decided to act, after years of near-constant fights, Greg's and my parting was smooth and incredibly cooperative. To this day, we remain friends. A friend told me years later, "I keep forgetting you were divorced. You don't carry it around like many others do," referring to bitterness and regret that many people harbor years after a divorce. Had I jumped out quickly, I would have done so without resolving my underlying lack of confidence in being on my own. While I can't know what exactly would have happened, the chances are high that I would have stumbled into another romantic relationship to compensate for that lack.

I learned there is a way to recover from negative outcomes of hasty action. One of them is to not rush into another hurried attempt at undoing. The other requires addressing the root causes that led to the action in the first place. Strategic inaction can be leveraged even after a hasty one for better future results. By the time I acted, after waiting for years, it felt like I had laid down the burden of doing. My decision to divorce, when it came, was natural and automatic. You might even call it inspired action.

MASTERING ACTION

We all have different life experiences, and yet we all experience similar pressures to act a certain way, conform with social norms, and do what it takes. The choice remains with us: We can either allow ourselves to be swept away with the "doingness" of our world or rise above it.

True mastery is about knowing when to act and when not to act. It is about recognizing that inspired action is far more productive and effective than urgent but misguided action and can lead to a better path to great results.

Just as a regular physical workout routine sets us up for making healthier eating choices throughout the day and week, I believe practicing thoughtful inaction in some areas helps build up that cognitive muscle, which then can help us make better choices throughout our day.

In later chapters, we will explore stories of others who have all grappled with their action bias and have come up with their own recipes to intercept or preempt their tendencies.

We will discover why we do what we do and what we can "do" to not do as much.

CONTEMPLATE

1. On a scale of one to five (five being the highest), where are you on the "too busy to think" spectrum these days?
2. Think of an aspect of life in which you tend to over prepare because of something that happened in the past. Does it serve you to be as over prepared now?

CHAPTER 3

THE RISE (AND IRONY) OF THE SELF-AWARENESS ERA

———

"Never confuse movement with action."

—ERNEST HEMINGWAY

Self-awareness can help intercept or preempt our action bias. In recent years, growing trends such as meditation and yoga have been helping develop this awareness. Ironically, we bring our action bias into this space too.

Sometimes we become aware of our action-oriented self-care choices soon enough. Jelena Jenzsch is a senior executive in consumer goods and a German native. In 2010, she took on a new job that came with significant changes to her professional and personal life. She moved from Bavaria in South Germany to Hamburg in the north.

Her role was to integrate an independently running business line into the main unit. The combined effect of moving cross country and working in a new company brought on stress. She told me, "I came from the outside and didn't have long-term connections like others did. And I was making big changes. It was a stressful time."

To deal with the stress of a new job and city, she turned to yoga for help. Surprisingly, she started to get sick after doing these yoga sessions and realized, "The yoga was too physical and exhausting. It was Ashtanga yoga, so it was very physically demanding. I realized that I have to slow down and address the mental aspect of my life. That's when I started to do meditation."

Jenzsch's first instinct was to turn to yoga to destress. But that too turned out to be full of action. Her body's response helped Jenzsch realize that what she needed to counter the mental stress of her job was not more physical activity but meditation, which works on the mind more directly than the body.

Her story reminded me of my own discovery of yoga. I had transitioned to management consulting in a new industry, e-commerce, and was flying every week to my client. I had enough awareness to realize all that travel and eating out wasn't good for me. I found a yoga class close to my client location and signed up. Yoga classes were few and far between in the Atlanta suburb where I worked back in 2006. After the first few sessions, I noticed we didn't seem to "do" much in class. We would stay in the same pose for minutes at a time. The teacher would walk around making micro-corrections to our pose. I started wondering, "Does she even know how to teach *real* yoga?" The only yoga I knew at the time was Vinyasa flow, which has constant movement. *That's* what I wanted. This particular form, Iyengar yoga, was a whole lot of nothing. It was slow and downright boring. My teacher would keep repeating things like "pull up your kneecaps," "pull down your shoulder blades," "lift your sternum." What on Earth are shoulder blades, I would wonder? (I eventually asked her. They are the triangular bones in the back of the shoulders. Keeping them pulled down during yoga prevents shoulder injury. In fact, pulling them down throughout the day can mitigate the stress we build up in our shoulders). I stayed in class for several months, partly because I couldn't find any other yoga class nearby and partly because these classes made a difference to my posture throughout the day.

It is possible to overdo even in yoga. A *Journal of Sports Medicine* research study on yoga injuries found sprains to be the most common kinds of injuries and that "excess effort" was one of the main causes of these injuries. People try too hard. The training in Atlanta, which I thought wasn't action-packed enough, helped me take better advantage of the faster forms of yoga later on, without injury. Today, years later, parts of my body, core, knees, shoulders, and sternum—autocorrect themselves when I am in a flow class. I can hear my first teacher's voice in my head even now.

Over the past ten years or so, phrases such as mindfulness and self-care have become mainstream American lifestyles. And yet, it is ironic that in the pursuit of self-awareness we bring the same action orientation that marks our regular life. Offshoots such as power yoga, hot yoga, and competitive yoga (which is quite an oxymoron in itself!) are modern innovations to the physical aspect of yoga. They are as physical and action packed as the lives we are seeking escape from. Even when we take the long overdue vacation, we come back exhausted from all the activity while vacationing. How many times have you said or heard someone say, "I need a vacation from my vacation"?

HOW TO APPLY ACTION BIAS TO
AN ANCIENT EASTERN SPIRITUAL PRACTICE

Is it not incongruous that sometimes, even in seeking relief from our action-filled lives, we make choices that introduce more action? Jenzsch's choice of active yoga and my disappointment with the slower form of yoga point to our tendency to gravitate toward action when we mean to give our bodies a break.

While some of us privately find our way to a balance through trial and error, others have been bold and vulnerable enough to publicly share their major breakdowns as a result of constant doing.

WHEN A BREAKDOWN LEADS TO A BREAKTHROUGH

Renée Dineen is, in her words, a "recovering workaholic and doing addict." In February 2020, she shared her story through a TEDx Talk "Authentic Inaction—Undoing the Doing in a Do-Crazy World," in which she chronicled her "doing addiction" and a health scare that served as a wakeup call. In 2015, following this health scare, she quit the major source of her action addiction, her high-paying executive job in biotech, cold turkey.

In calling it an addiction, her choice of words was interesting. She told me, "I called it an addiction because my 'doing life' had me. I did not have it. 'Doing addicts' are honored and encouraged. It is a behavior that is even expected, an identity rooted in our culture. There's this affirmation that comes through that addiction, as opposed to the shaming that comes with other addictions. This is what also keeps it in place." Her phrasing must have struck a chord. Her TEDx Talk is at nearly 600,000 views.

A couple of years before quitting, she was enjoying one of her highs by leading a major organizational transformation at a biotech firm. While that was going on, she was approached by a senior executive who wanted her to take the lead on another transformation in his organization. She felt tempted and pressured at the same time. The other transformation was bigger, impacting 14,000 people, and had more visibility. She had her doubts and misgivings; the previous transformation wasn't complete and the why for this new opportunity wasn't clear. But the vice president (VP) who approached her was persuasive. Dineen agreed to transition.

What followed was a grueling eighteen-month period with international travel every six weeks, long hours, and canceled family holidays. In the meantime, the team she left behind became leaderless and the transformation faltered. After about a year and a half, before the new initiative was completed, the VP retired. Since this transformation was his baby, it became orphaned and petered out. "I didn't get to finish either transformation," says Dineen with regret.

By then she had also developed severe health symptoms: tremors and stutters. Her doctors thought she had MS (multiple sclerosis, a disease of the brain and spinal cord) but tests and scans came back negative. This was her wakeup call. "It was at that point I knew that my own 'undoing' would require me to make some significant life changes. Others may not require this level of change, but I did. I needed to completely shift the flow of my day-to-day life and commit myself to coming into greater alignment with who I was and what I really wanted to do." She quit.

Today, Dineen is an author, motivational speaker, and a leadership and lifestyle coach. Perhaps Dineen needed a major breakdown to reach her ultimate breakthrough. Hopefully, the rest of us don't wait until we get that kind of wakeup call. This story is a reminder that action addiction could become a real thing for each of us; the high we get from doing and outcomes makes us want to chase more action for the next high, much like other forms of better understood addictions.

The more ambitious and successful we are, the more we thrive on action. Even when we choose a break, we tend to make action-filled choices. As you consider your life, on the spectrum of choices made by Jenzsch and Dineen, where would you like to see yourself? Where are you headed?

How do we avoid getting to the point of burnout? Parts two and three of this book address how the pursuit of results turns into a mindless pursuit of action and how we can overcome some of the addiction builders. Here, we will explore one mitigating solution that is popular but, in my mind, yet to be fully utilized.

MINDFULNESS AND MEDITATION: GOING DEEPER THAN THE TREND

In recent years, mindfulness and meditation practices have been growing exponentially. However, I notice many people are unable or unwilling to commit to these practices on an ongoing basis. I have discovered that their action bias gets in the way of adopting these practices, keeping them deprived of their full benefits.

My own journey to fully embracing these practices was a slow one. Growing up in the fast-paced big-city life of Mumbai, yoga and meditation were not part of normal life for me. Having extensively read about the downfall of the famous Indian Guru Osho in the 1980s, I was skeptical of all self-styled gurus who often teach meditation. Since then, I have come to appreciate the teachings of Osho, but the scandals during his life made me distrustful of the so-called spiritual path. While I knew the story of Buddha, I didn't know any practicing Buddhists. I wasn't sold on any of this stuff.

Nonetheless, I was convinced by my sister to attend a breathwork and meditation workshop in 2008. In this workshop they asked us to ponder these questions: Who are you, what are you, and where are you? I had been a self-declared atheist since I was nine. While I am no longer as black and white on atheism, I consider myself (and did then) a logical, analytical, and scientific person. All this sounded like mind games—a bunch of tish-tash hogwash. But I decided to give it a fair trial and diligently did my daily breathwork practices. I had researched it enough to feel confident it wasn't voodoo. Over time, what convinced me was the positive effect these practices had in my own daily life experience. That practice evolved and broadened into a study of Vedic and Buddhist philosophies and is by now an integrated part of how I think and live life. I wrote an article called "Journey of a Skeptic" in 2011 chronicling my evolution on the path.

Yoga and meditation retreats have become a major business. *The Wall Street Journal* reported that for Generation X (born between 1965–1980), the solution for their middle-age crisis has evolved from buying sports cars and other material pursuits to yoga and meditation retreats. A 2020 meditation market research report projects the global meditation business to grow to nine billion dollars by 2027, with two billion in the United States in 2020 alone. Now that's big business! According to a *Quartz* report, more than 2,500 meditation apps launched between 2015 and 2021. As I looked for research on the effectiveness of these apps, I found a lot of conflicting or limited studies. It was fascinating to see some studies claiming meditation and mental health apps as effective in reducing stress and other reports questioning the methods of these studies.

My interest in watching this industry and the adoption of the meditation trend comes from the fact that I co-founded a meditation initiative, well before it became a hot trend. In 2011, I worked with fellow professional New Yorkers to launch a meditation program called *I Meditate New York*. As we did marketing brainstorms on how to message the benefits, we realized that promoting it as a tool along the lines of "slow down and smell the roses" wasn't going to fly with busy and ambitious New Yorkers who are wired to move fast. So, we came up with a clever slogan: "Meditation helps you go faster in life, by slowing down for twenty minutes a day." Our slogan worked back then; we launched the initiative at a 2,700-person meditation event at Lincoln Center in Manhattan, and the service is still running.

Despite the popularity of meditation, too many people don't get the full benefits of this practice. I notice many people give meditation a try because it's popular but also give up on it quickly. Common complaints I've heard are "I can't keep my mind steady. I can't sit still. I get too many thoughts" and so on. They blame themselves: "My mind just goes very fast."

You see, when you meditate, you come face-to-face with a paradox. The goal of meditation, seemingly, is to get to a "no-thought" state. The apparent promise is that you will become like the peaceful-looking model in the ad, sitting upright, wearing fancy yoga gear and a gentle, blissful smile.

WHAT WE THINK
SHOULD HAPPEN
DURING MEDITATION

WHAT ACTUALLY
HAPPENS DURING
MEDITATION

And yet, the moment we sit down in meditation, thoughts come flooding to the mind. An itch develops somewhere on the body. The room feels too hot or too cold. An irritating click-clack sound comes from somewhere. *It feels like a mess.* You scratch your leg, and the itch comes right back on the arm. You shift to get comfortable, and the pain returns a little later. The irony of meditation is the more you do something to try to get to that no-thought stage, the more it becomes elusive.

When new meditators struggle with all this, they feel that they have failed. Maybe this is not for them. They give up.

What they don't realize is that the thoughts and discomfort were always present in their mind-body system. Meditation merely gave their system a chance to release it. The practice of meditation is the practice of allowing thoughts and releasing them versus suppressing them by, say, binge watching TV. Meditation is the practice of noticing it all: the itch, the thoughts, the sound of your neighbor's noisy breathing. It's the practice of noticing your discomfort with all of that. And it is the practice of *doing absolutely nothing about it*. For action-oriented people, this is a hard thing to accept.

I am reminded of advice my mother used to give me. I have an older brother who was a prankster as a young boy. Since I was the only younger sibling he had, I was often the target of his teasing and pranks. I would try to fight back or outsmart him, lose, and then complain to our mother. She would tell me, "Why do you get irritated? Just ignore him; he will get bored and go away." Alas, I never took her advice, and our sibling bickering went on.

Turns out, her advice applies to our minds too. The paradox within the paradox (!) is that the moment we notice the thoughts or itch or pain and don't react, we diffuse the effect of that irritant. It goes away on its own.

When I was writing this book, I discovered an unexpected connection between meditation and writer's block. At that time, I attended a private talk by author Daniel Pink who was addressing the so-called writer's block or "a psychological inhibition preventing a writer from proceeding with a piece" as defined by *Merriam-Webster*. Pink believes that there is no such thing as a writer's block; "it is only your unwillingness to sit down and write crappy stuff."

Like writer's block, meditation is not difficult. It is only our unwillingness to sit down and deal with the crappy-thinking nature of our mind. I learned when writing this book that the only way through writer's block is to write. I learned in the early years of meditation that the only way to deal with the mental and physical crap that comes up during meditation is to meditate.

A regular meditation practice is the best, low-risk way of practicing non-doing. No apps and props are needed; you and your breath are enough. If you can breathe, you can meditate. As someone who has been practicing for a while now, I can attest that the struggle never fully goes away. I still catch myself saying, "I had a really good (or bad) meditation today," even though I know that the label of good or bad is purely my mind comparing the experience to a made-up image of what meditation *should* be like. There is a reason why it's called a practice. It has no end result, no goals to achieve, no real outcome to strive for, other than just being with it—"it" being whatever comes during the meditation. When we sit in meditation, we are, in reality, practicing overcoming our action bias, our mental triggers.

Meditation is not a skill but a habit to be developed. It is an excellent way to practice inaction in the smallest micro-moments, where the stakes are not so high, which can then serve as training for inaction as a choice in the bigger moments of life.

In the next part of the book, we will look into the major obstacles in daily life that can worsen our action bias and what strategic and thoughtful inaction might look like in those situations.

CONTEMPLATE

1. Can you think of a time in the past when you wanted to give yourself a break and landed up more aggravated or busy? Can you laugh at the irony in the choices you made?

2. What reasons do you like to give for not meditating regularly? If you do have a regular practice, how would you answer the question "How's your practice going". Notice any judgment or analysis creeping into your answer.

PART 2

DEALING WITH OBSTACLES TO MASTERING ACTION

CHAPTER 4

THE DEFAULT ACTION PLAYBOOK

———

"If you see a bandwagon, it's too late."

—JAMES GOLDSMITH

"Couldn't we get her out of there? Obviously, she has some kind of mental problem." This was one of the many complaints sent by a concerned employee to their senior management.

Pilvi Takala is a Finnish artist whose medium is candid camera. In one of her social experiments, she was "hired" as a trainee by the marketing department at a European office of Deloitte, a major global consulting company. In this job, she chose to spend her days in open layout office areas, without a computer or phone. She would sit there staring into nothing, seemingly thinking. She would take her meal breaks and return to staring into empty space, still thinking. When asked what she was doing, she would reply, "I am doing brain work for my thesis." She was polite and had a good story to tell: She was a trainee in the marketing department and was writing a thesis on global brands. She described her working style to her colleagues: "We always use the computer all day but from time to time I try to manage everything without a machine." One day she rode the elevator up and down, never getting off. And when people inquired, she would answer, "I like riding the elevator; it helps me think. It's like being on a train. I always have such good thoughts on trains, so I thought I might try that here."

Within a couple of days, the reaction of her colleagues went from mild curiosity to amusement to downright hostility. This was followed by complaints to the higher-ups. The leadership team, which was in on the experiment, replied to all complaints assuring everyone that her thesis was coming along very well. Her behavior was not affecting her work or performance. This didn't help the people around her who grew increasingly alarmed. Two days later, a voicemail left for her manager went like this: "So now she is lodging in the elevator…and riding back and forth with people…I don't want to go into the same elevator with her." Another email read, "…People spend senseless amount of time speculating this issue. Couldn't we get her out of there? Obviously she has some kind of mental problem."

Takala's colleagues equated her "thinking" at work with a mental problem. The fact that she didn't behave like others, busy working away at her computer, made her seem unproductive and downright odd.

Many employers have a different problem with unproductivity in the workplace. A *New York Post* research study found that employees spend as much as eight hours a week on non-work activities such as online shopping or "watching last night's Yankees or Mets game." They appear busy because they are looking at a screen, but they are not contributing to their work. In the mid-2000s retailers noticed an interesting trend of people shopping online—from the office on the Monday after Thanksgiving—and gave it a name: Cyber Monday. In 2020, customers spent a record 10.2 billion dollars globally on Cyber Monday, when they were supposed to be working.

The difference between someone surreptitiously wasting time at work and Takala's behavior is the appearance of things. We look busy when we stare at the computer for hours, regardless of what we are doing. We look like we have a mental problem when we stare into empty space, even if it leads to creative ideas (as we shall see when we learn about mind-wandering and daydreaming in chapter 10). It is more important for us to fit in and follow the default action playbook even if it costs us productivity and results.

BLAME IT ON NORM THEORY

Our tendency to follow the norm and do what's expected is an indirect cause of our action bias and isn't limited to awkward office situations. In a research study of physicians, published in the *Journal of Family Practice*, a group of doctors were presented with hypothetical cases listing patient symptoms that they could not easily diagnose. They were asked to make their recommendations based on the symptoms that had been described. A large majority of the physicians recommended tests and procedures, which we can call "action." A very small minority chose a wait-and-watch approach, which is equivalent to inaction, not doing anything. In real life from where these cases were derived, the patients' symptoms had gone away with time and without any medical intervention.

You see, when a patient comes to a doctor with a problem, there is an expectation that the doctor will do something about it. It is the norm for the physician to take action. That expectation creates a compulsion for the doctor to, well, do something, anything, even prescribe additional tests, whether they are needed or not. It gives everyone a sense of comfort that they did something about it, even if it created wasted effort, not to mention the expense of unnecessary tests.

The tendency to default to an action playbook is a human quality, and it exists where humans operate. I find sports to be a treasure trove of data and research on human behavior and psychology. A research study published in *Journal of Economic Psychology* analyzed penalty kicks in soccer. Penalty kicks lead to a score about 80 percent of the time. A scored penalty kick means the goalkeeper failed to achieve their desired outcome, which is to catch the ball. This study measured penalty kicks in top leagues and championships worldwide and plotted a probability distribution of kick direction.

Given the likelihood of the kick direction, the study concluded that the ideal position for goalkeepers was to stay in the goal's center and not move. In reality, goalkeepers almost always jumped left or right in anticipation of the kick. In this context, they took action. And by doing so, they missed the chance of catching the ball.

Why on Earth would someone do something that leads to a negative result?

ACTION BIAS IN SOCCER PENALTY KICKS

The data the researchers collected in the study included surveys asking the goalkeepers and coaches about their state of mind and decision making. They found that the norm for goalkeepers in penalty kicks is to act (jump to the right or to the left); it's just what they do. They found that taking the action of jumping gave them a sense of being able to control the outcome, as if their "doing something" will help them with their goal of catching the ball.

Moreover, regret, a direct trigger of our action bias, played a role here. If the goalkeeper took action (jumped) and a goal was still scored, he could give himself a hall pass because he took his best shot. On the other hand, if he didn't do anything (did not jump) and a goal was scored, he experienced regret. In his mind, he could have done something about it.

Remember Mahesh Kothurkar from chapter 2 who ignored the fire alarm on his aircraft carrier and lived to regret it? It made him excessively biased toward action in the future, causing him to pay the price with anxiety and stress. Regret has a powerful effect on us and can make us do things that don't serve us.

Shall we blame our psychological wiring then? That is certainly an option. Or we can consider rewiring our tendencies in those aspects of our lives and work that matter.

PLAYBOOK FOR A CRISIS

It started out as any other day for Singh. He was in his second year as CEO of the global oncology division of a multinational medical technology company, which develops imaging, therapy, and technology solutions to study and treat cancers. This day, however, was to be interrupted by a phone call. A four-year-old child had died in a hospital while on a machine made by his division.

Crisis management is a major field of study in business. From my experience in management roles at large businesses, companies have a playbook to handle expected crises. Crises require fast decision making; these playbooks are well understood and senior leaders well versed with them. Death of a patient is one such possibility for a health care company, and they have a playbook to deal with it. Singh shared it with me. "Step 1: Call the lawyer. Step 2: Issue a gag order to all employees. Step 3: Direct your engineers to conduct a post-facto investigation. Call your boss," and so on.

So, what did Singh do? He told his administrative assistant, "I am going for a walk," and left. He walked for two hours. Wasn't that risky? I asked him. "Yes, there was a risk. What if a lawyer [for the other side] had called? What if a journalist called? People may have thought I was abandoning them. If you don't share information during a crisis, people make up their own information."

What made him decide to go for a walk in spite of those risks? "I knew I had a good [leadership] team who would hold the fort. I knew that eventually I would hear the thoughts of others. I would get advice. But I wanted to take some time before I contaminated my mind with all these thoughts. I wanted to become conversant with this situation, which is a once-in-a-lifetime situation for a CEO."

"I came to a decision pretty early in the walk. I was not going to put out a gag order or lawyer up—none of the nonsense that is endemic in large companies," Singh said. He decided, instead, that he would fly to the scene of the incident.

I asked him whether he assessed his options before arriving at the decision. He replied, "I didn't run an Excel sheet of pros and cons in my head." He already knew of the worst-case outcomes. "We might have to shut down the unit, and we might have to sign a consent decree with the FDA," referring to a voluntary, final, and binding settlement with the Food and Drug Administration. This would include a series of measures the company would take before resuming operations. "If we survive, there will be a lot of learnings. But we could also die in the process."

So, what was the deciding factor? "I was trying to answer the question: What would I do if it was my family member? What would *I* do for the family of the child?"

Singh flew out to meet with the hospital administrators. He took one scientist with him. No lawyer. No public relations executive. "I was aware that just because I was taking a nonlegal approach, there was no guarantee they would do the same."

After two days, the CEO of the hospital agreed to meet him. They agreed to cooperate and investigate the incident together. Four days later the postmortem report indicated the child had suffered a massive cardiac arrest. The machine was not the cause of death. "That didn't change anything for me," says Singh. He had flown to be there for the family, so he stayed on. He had another request for the CEO. "Could I meet with the parents?" The hospital got consent from the single mother who invited Singh to coffee. At coffee, there was no discussion of machines and science. He asked the mom if she would consider visiting his company and sharing her experience with his team. After an initial hesitation, she agreed and flew to the company's offices in California. A thousand people at Singh's townhall meeting heard her story and experience. At the end, Singh had a simple reminder for his team: "Please understand what happens on the other side of what we do. Please understand that there could be a child at the end of that beam that comes out of the machine we build."

Looking back, Singh believes that series of events had more impact on the quality consciousness of the company than any amount of Six Sigma training (a well-established program designed to improve the quality of the products manufactured by a business. It can cost thousands of dollars per employee to implement). "I didn't have to create a quality program for people on the shop floor. After that meeting, they got together, built extra testing protocols, and added a third shift."

Singh wasn't avoiding the problem; he leveraged the power of strategic inaction. He had confidence in this team's ability to handle any unexpected developments, like a phone call from a journalist looking for breaking news, while he was out. Going for a walk gave him time to preempt the effect of worldly advice that was bound to create conflict between principles and playbook. He wasn't being irresponsible. If anything, his subsequent actions reveal a greater sense of responsibility toward patients and their families. The actual path to great results, which included improving quality on the production floor, was nonlinear.

A particular risk in not following the default action path is social censure and rejection. The world demands decisive action or at least the appearance of it. "What are you going to *do* about it?" "I am going to take a walk" is not considered an acceptable answer, certainly not in the middle of a crisis. The decisions Singh made came from his principles, not from a default action playbook. His principles enabled him to take the risk of social censure which often accompanies high-visibility decisions.

In Singh's case, he had support from his team as well as people he reported to. After this incident was over, he got a "slap on the wrist" from the legal department for the risk he took. His senior leadership aligned with his decisions, which were made from principles. One way to handle the risk from failing to keep up appearances is to have the key stakeholders on your side. In Takala's case, her colleagues were not on her side. She was too new and hadn't built her support structure yet. Fortunately for her, the whole thing was an experiment. She had nothing to lose.

Standing for principles is a tricky business. You can get burned at the stake for it, or you can become a hero. You need a certain appetite for risk to stand for your principles, especially if it means going against the norm or your own deepest instinct to do something.

In many of my interviews with people who chose not to follow the default action path in the context of their situation, the word *principles* was to come up again and again.

CONTEMPLATE

1. Have you ever launched on an action path just because that was the norm (or you were under pressure) and later realized that wasn't the best path to take? Could you have chosen differently?
2. Is there anything going on in your life right now where it's worth rethinking the actions you have been taking?

CHAPTER 5

A PRINCIPLES-BASED ACTION PLAYBOOK

———

"Pain + Reflection = Progress"

—RAY DALIO, *PRINCIPLES*

We are not born with principles. While we can read books on principles written by successful people (American investor Ray Dalio has written one), sometimes the best way is to let life teach you a lesson, which then helps develop and internalize a principle. I learned my own lesson in following the default action playbook early in my retail career. All names were changed in the next story.

It was 2010. I had just left the windowless office of my human resources (HR) partner. We had met to discuss an employee I managed whose role was being terminated due to an organizational change. My HR partner was clear and articulate in describing all the steps in this role termination. This was clearly not her first rodeo. And yet, I was disturbed. I couldn't get rid of the feeling we were doing this wrong. I had shared my concerns in the meeting. Her response? "This ship has sailed. The role termination paperwork is almost ready. You need to execute the plan." As I walked away from her office, I told myself uneasily, *If other, more experienced people than me think this is the right thing to do, then maybe it is.*

I was working for an e-commerce division of a large retailer. Business had been great for years. It was about to get better. Our leadership had announced a bold new plan of doubling revenue in three years. As part of the new direction, I had taken on a newly created role and was working on my vision of using analytics to help drive newer business models. I was both excited and nervous. I had thus far been successful in building new technology for the company. This was to be my first foray into business and sales modeling. I was a technologist, not a modeler. I would need a team of people better at modeling and statistics than me. I had been a people manager for three years, and this would be my first time building a new team and skill set from scratch.

My new role came with a team of two junior employees who had Excel reporting skills. I inherited them from my new manager. In sharing the plan for the two associates, he told me that one of them, Elizabeth, didn't have the skills to transition to the new team and that a decision had been made to terminate her employment citing "organizational redesign." The other employee, Angie, had transferable skills and would be transitioned into a new role reporting to me. I had been promised a bigger headcount as we got deeper into the growth cycle. He urged me, "The faster you backfill Elizabeth, the faster you can deliver and hire even more people."

I got on the job of paperwork to terminate Elizabeth's role. This was my first time terminating an employment. The process seemed simple and well established. But the situation turned out not to be as simple. I quickly noticed that Elizabeth was a poor performer, failing to deliver basic reports. The feedback from others was unanimous. She had not performed well since she joined a little over a year ago. People found her mannerism unfriendly, and they felt their input and feedback on her work was ignored as the same issues showed up again and again. I told my manager, "This is not a role termination case; this is a performance problem that was never addressed."

In most organizations, following a performance management plan to address underperforming employees can take months. My manager, a high-energy, fast-talking, sharp man assured me that role termination was the faster and more efficient route. "The faster you let her go, the quicker you can hire into that headcount. You need to get going here." The message was clear. Speed mattered. It was in the DNA of the company.

Things were moving fast elsewhere. As I sat in the boardroom, our largest meeting room where the big guns met, I listened to other leaders walk through their fancy slides overflowing with aggressive and bold ideas. I envied them their well-thought-out quarterly and seasonal plans, which would contribute to the ambitious sales and margin targets. Here I was, with not even a team in place. Every now and then, my manager would look in my direction. "Jinny is putting a team together to help us build better projections. We will have more clear sales and margin plans for this idea then." As all eyes turned to me, the confident smile on my face belied the fact that I felt I was far from fulfilling that promise.

Meanwhile, things were not going so well on the recruiting front. I was struggling to hire talent for this unique, part-technical, part-merchant planner, part-statistician skill set. My recruiting team was accustomed to hiring traditional retail merchant roles, and it was taking them time to learn how to recruit for these new kinds of roles. This forced me to get more involved in the process.

The pressure was on. With so much on my plate, I decided to get going with the role termination. Elizabeth was first surprised, then angry. "The company is growing, so how can you terminate my role? You need to find me another job." We went through the process of her applying for other jobs. Knowing her performance and behavioral issues, no one in the broader team could recommend her. In our rush to take action, we hadn't been honest about our reasons for terminating her role. Had she been a good performer, the collective team would have found something for her. We were hiring in many other parts of the company. At some level, I believe, our inauthenticity showed. On the last day of her employment, as she left, her parting words were bitter: "I will never have anything to do with this company again." We had lost goodwill. We had also lost a customer.

In my pursuit of speed and results, I was following a default playbook. We all were. It is common practice in corporations to weed out less desirable team members under the guise of organizational redesign. When faced with tough situations it is often easiest and most effective to follow the norm, the default playbook. Following the default playbook has its virtues; we have support from the large majority that believes in that action path. I paid no price in my career growth at the company for my actions. In fact, I had plenty of support from all my stakeholders, including human resources.

Playbooks save us time and effort so we don't have to reinvent the wheel. But the very nature of the playbook leads us to a default path that everyone else is following toward the same results. It quickly becomes unoriginal. Often, we give up our own instincts in favor of how everyone else is doing it. Especially when the "everyone elses" are bosses, advisors, mentors, and even our heroes whose tweets we hang on to. And yet, for every established playbook, someone tried it first to achieve new heights of success. Following an off-playbook path can lead to greater success through nonlinear paths, as we will see when we revisit this story a little later.

Another downside of following the default playbook is missed opportunities, especially in the world of innovation.

THE STARTUP FOUNDER'S PLAYBOOK

A year or so before I was learning my lesson, Wharton professor and author Adam Grant was about to learn his. A student came to him and asked Grant to invest in his company. The student said, "I'm working with three friends, and we're going to try to disrupt an industry by selling stuff online."

Grant said, "Okay, you guys spent the whole summer on this, right?"

"No, we all took internships just in case it doesn't work out."

"All right, but you're going to go in full time once you graduate."

"Not exactly. We've all lined up backup jobs."

Months went by. The day before the company was to launch, it had no functioning website. This company was going to sell stuff online.

Grant declined to invest.

The business his students launched is called Warby Parker, a successful disruptor of the eyewear industry with a revenue of 250 million dollars in 2019.

We love stories of entrepreneurs who gave up everything to single-mindedly pursue their vision. Especially glamorous are stories where the founder invested "every last penny" on his new venture, living in the basement (or couch) of friends and family. These tales bring forth the image of strong and brave "action figures" we grew up worshipping. But not everyone was designed to be an action figure. And being an action figure isn't the only path to great success.

The founders of Warby Parker didn't follow the startup founder playbook. They didn't conform. It was indeed easy to dismiss them. Grant shared this story in his 2016 TED Talk, "The Surprising Habits of Original People." He joked that his wife now manages their investments.

It takes something to challenge the norm and default action plan and to create an original approach. Subsequently, the rewards can be outsized. Many years ago, I had made an unusual and risky bet on an emerging technology, leading to great success. A colleague remarked to me then: "No one ever got fired for buying an IBM [considered a safe bet for many decades], but no one got promoted for it either."

APPLYING NEWLY DEVELOPED PRINCIPLES

Back at the e-commerce division where I was working, I was moving on from the matter of Elizabeth. I had recently hired a promising young woman with prior merchandising and planning background. It quickly became apparent, however, that we had overestimated her skill set during interviews. My HR partner told me about a ninety-day probationary period during which I could terminate a new hire's employment with no cause, saving me from the extensive performance plan process, which could take months. Once again, speed was of the essence, and here was a way out. We were going even faster now; work was coming in quicker than I could handle.

But I had learned my lesson. This time, I refused to act on what looked like the fastest and most efficient route. Instead, I had long developmental conversations with my new hire, Latricia. I promised her I would support her with everything I had, but I needed her to step up. Her Excel skills were woefully inadequate. She couldn't answer questions about her planning assumptions in meetings. I shared my surprise at her skills, considering her prior background working as a merchandise planner. "I can get you training. I will provide you air cover, but I can't be in every meeting with you. You need to pull your weight."

After a month of frequent and candid conversations, there was no improvement and I informed Latricia I had no choice but proceed with a performance plan. It was personally disappointing. Here was a bright and eager young woman, who had moved cross country to fulfill her dream of living in New York City. It was heartbreaking to see her trying hard and failing. A couple of weeks later, Latricia acknowledged my feedback and told me this was not a good culture fit for her. She opted to leave immediately with a severance package. We parted ways on good terms.

A few weeks later, I got an unexpected email from Latricia. She was doing well and had transitioned into career and life coaching. She suggested her friend for another role I was hiring for. I interviewed her friend, Natasha, and hired her. Natasha turned out to be one of my best hires, dealing with some of the trickiest political and organizational problems with intelligence and grace. She stayed with the company for many years, growing into senior roles over time.

When I rushed through a role termination, driven by urgency and a misguided need for speed, my actions were legally above board and compatible with the existing norm. But they were less humane. The second time around, I operated from my principle of supporting my team and being transparent with them. I chose not to take the default action and spent the time working with my direct report, not around her. I landed at the same outcome: parting ways. But by leveraging the power of strategic inaction, I unearthed an unexpected silver lining. Latricia was with us long enough to learn the inner workings, pace, and culture better than even my recruiter. My company, team, and I not only didn't lose goodwill, but we also saved time in recruiting for the great talent that she sent us as her gift. The path to great results was nonlinear; so were the results. Moreover, I developed a habit of transparency in dealing with colleagues, especially those reporting to me, which was to help me in the years to come.

Sometimes a particular default action or playbook may seem like the fastest way. But a thoughtful pause to apply your principles filter can bring forth ideas that yield far better and more powerful results than default action. The rewards of strategic inaction can be outsized. Singh's decision, in chapter 4, to not act before aligning with his value system and principles sent a clear signal to employees, partners, and stakeholders on what matters: the patient and their family. He also saved money on external training programs; his team was inspired to improve the quality of their processes. By giving themselves time and a financial cushion through a paying job, Warby Parker's founders took unnecessary pressure off themselves to create something original and long lasting. That time allowed them to perfect the customer experience for something that no one could have imagined buying online: spectacles. These off-playbook choices led to better, unexpected business results than any amount of following the playbook might have. This might mean risking social censure, even from our colleagues, bosses, loved ones, and mentors. But the rewards of giving ourselves enough pause to find out how *we* want to approach our goals and trusting our unique method are priceless.

CONTEMPLATE

1. Have you ever stood for your principles and failed to get agreement from those who mattered? Have you ever stood for principles, and people who disagreed at first eventually turned around to support you? What was the difference between those situations? What did you learn?
2. Is there anything coming up in your life right now that is worth running your plan through a principles filter?

CHAPTER 6

PRINCIPLES VS. GOALS

———

"I have concentrated all along on building the finest retailing company that we possibly could. Period. Creating a huge personal fortune was never particularly a goal of mine."

—SAM WALTON (FOUNDER OF WALMART),

NET WORTH IN 2021: $16.2 BILLION

A TALE OF TWO INVESTORS

The S&P 500, a benchmark to measure the stock market performance of the 500 largest US companies, was up more than 50 percent. A sense of exuberance was palpable in the market. Unemployment was under control. A new president had been elected, bringing a change to the political party in the White House.

Warren Buffett, an investor, had had a tremendous run thus far. The investment fund he managed had returned a compounded annual growth of 29.5 percent, which was many times the growth in all available benchmarks of that time, making him and his investors very rich. Early in his career, he had embraced investment principles from his mentor Benjamin Graham. Graham believed in an "intrinsic business value," a measure of a company's true worth totally independent of the stock price. Buffett had stuck to Graham's investment philosophy, called value investing, throughout his career, ignoring all other investing fads of the day.

Now, he was concerned with what was going on in the market.

The latest market upswing was being driven by a new kind of investor who didn't seem to be operating by principles. These new investors were causing stock prices to go up way beyond intrinsic business value. He couldn't find the value bargains he looked for in this "seemingly barren investment world."

Does this sound like 2020? It isn't. It is early 1969. What came to be called the go-go bull market of 1966–68 was about to lead to a bear market that would last a year and a half, causing the S&P to drop 35 percent from its peak in November 1968 to May 1970.

Bull and bear markets are terms used to describe the behavior of the stock market. In a bull market, the prices keep rising for an extended period of time, usually months or years, driven by a demand greater than the supply. In a bear market, the prices continue to decline for an extended period, driven by more stocks available than the demand for them.

In this case, Buffett was concerned that the increase in stock prices was not driven by sound investment principles. He was to be proven right when the market declined soon after. But before that happened, he was to make a radical decision.

At the height of his successful investment career, Buffett announced he was going to "retire." He was shutting down his investment fund. In a letter to his investors, he said, "A swelling interest in investment performance has created an increasingly short-term oriented and (in my opinion) more speculative market." As much as he was critical of the behavior of the market, he also seemed to be doubting himself. "Maybe I am merely suffering from a lack of mental flexibility," he said in his letter. He seemed influenced by an observer, commenting on security analysts over forty, who had stated, "They know too many things that are no longer true." Buffett was thirty-nine at the time.

While developing this book, I had become interested in the interplay between principles and goals. While a lot has been written about Buffett, this phase in his early career points to an interesting use of inaction in the life of someone whose entire profession is designed around the goal of making money. To dig deeper into his choices during this period, I spoke to Phil Terry, an author, entrepreneur, and a Buffett historian of sorts. Terry commented, "It was unprecedented, unheard of. He shut down his successful fund at the top of the market. Top of the market!" Perhaps someone observing Buffett back then might have thought he was giving up entirely, that he was calling it quits.

In the 1969 letter to his investors, Buffett anticipated a question. "Some of you are going to ask, 'What do you plan to do?' I don't have an answer to that question."

Contrary to his outwardly busy and productive life until then, he went on to do a bunch of nothing for the next couple of years. He managed the capital allocation for a small textiles business called Berkshire but had no operating responsibility. He started a peer discussion group, called Graham Group. He didn't seem very busy. By the time he emerged from this phase of apparent inactivity, he had been convinced by his partner Charlie Munger's advice to "switch from buying fair companies at wonderful prices, [a strategy he called cigar butt investing] to wonderful companies at fair prices."

Terry told me, "By 1972 he had undergone a transformation of his own thinking. And he left behind his cigar butt investing." He was to start the next blazing phase of his career, starting with See's Candies, investing in companies with a great management track record and customer service.

The two-year period of outwardly doing nothing served to transform Buffett's investment strategy. The path to this new strategy was nonlinear, and it made him even more wildly successful in the decades that followed. Today, he is considered one of the most successful investors and businesspeople, with a net worth of 102 billion dollars as of mid-2021.

In 2019, I got a personal glimpse of Buffett at his company Berkshire Hathaway's Shareholder Conference, which I attended as part of a leadership workshop organized by Terry. The impression I got of Buffett is that he is a man of inaction. You don't get the feel of hurry or urgency in his being. He sat there, addressing 40,000 people, as if he was in his living room chatting with a bunch of friends. Seven-year-old children asked him questions, as if they were talking to Grandpa Warren—no Wall Street action-packed pulsating energy here. He drank a lot of Coke and ate a lot of See's candy. When back home, he read books all day. And newspapers. He didn't seem to "do" much.

I was curious to know more about the mind of an investor and how they find the balance between buying/selling stocks versus waiting. Since I didn't have direct access to Buffett to pepper him with questions, I turned to Nitin Bhambhani, a managing director and equity analyst of twenty-six years at JP Morgan, a leading global financial firm. His job is to analyze technology companies and provide recommendations, which other investors in his group typically follow to make buy/sell decisions. The balance he needs to find is between expanding coverage to include more companies and in-depth analysis on each of them. The ultimate goal here is for investors who follow his picks to make money via buy/sell decisions on these stocks. What is visible to other investors is the breadth of companies in the system. What is visible to him is the complexity and depth of each company's operations and performance. The struggle between action and inaction, adding or not adding more companies, is a constant reality for him.

"I've made a lot of money for the firm by picking the right stocks. But then there are a bunch of stocks that I haven't covered that have gone up even more." Bhambhani's sector, technology, makes it more challenging. It's a constantly changing space with newer companies coming up rapidly. "To stay relevant, you have to cover newer companies. Otherwise, you become like the older companies: irrelevant." What does this conflict do to his state of mind? "I feel like I am in hell. I am always trying to cover new stuff, and it never ends. It's not a pleasant place to be."

How does he overcome the mental conflict? "My measure of success is not where I will be in the organization in the next five years. Or how much money I will make in the next five years. My measure of success is whether I've understood this company well. Have I been a value-added partner to them? I like to make money. I want to be successful. But I try to stay true to my objectives. I am almost a slave to my objectives."

The similarity between Buffett and Bhambhani is they are both in the business of making money, but they make active choices to not follow the default action path (which their competition may be doing). It is not that they are not active players. They are choosing to not hustle and chase money through a lot of action: buying and selling. They are not playing the numbers game. They have made a lot of money for themselves and others. But they don't get caught up in their money-making goals at the expense of their principles and long-term objectives.

They have also both experienced self-doubt. At thirty-nine, Buffet was concerned about his "mental flexibility." Bhambhani talks of "mental hell." They are as susceptible to doubting their choice to not participate in herd acting as the rest of us. How do they make the conflict go away? I don't think they ever do. They just ignore the voice in their head and stick to acting from their principles.

As I interviewed others for this book, and in my own experience, many who have overcome their action bias in specific areas of their life and work are still susceptible to the voice in their head that tempts them to a default action path. Conflict, guilt, and self-doubt are a part of their journey as much as ours. What helps them get past doubt and conflict is that they put their principles above all else. All sorts of wonderful opportunities open up if you arrest the impulse to act and allow time for inspired action to show up.

However, principles alone won't help if the goals themselves are misaligned with the principles. And some people, especially the very young, have not yet developed a robust set of principles.

IT ALL STARTS WITH GOAL SETTING

A major indirect cause of our action bias lies in the way we set and pursue goals. Goal setting is an intrinsic part of human behavior and a necessary tool to drive progress. However, the goal-setting process for most of us inherently leads to incomplete goals. Our tendency to pursue our goals creates the compounding effect of chasing action while chasing outcomes based on flawed and incomplete goals. Sometimes, though, life teaches us to broaden our goals.

As a child of immigrant parents, Anu Sethi grew up with an ambitious life plan. She was always an A-plus student and was salutatorian in high school. She got accepted to all the colleges she applied to and finally chose Columbia Barnard College. She was a top performer at her first job with Morgan Stanley in New York City. A few years into her career, she completed her part-time MBA and switched to a job with Booz & Company, one of the top-tier global management consulting firms, in New York City. The goal was clear in Sethi's mind: "In six years I'm going to make a partner or principal. Then I'll get poached by a firm as their head of a function or strategy group. And that's it; my career would be set."

Why the specific route of management consulting? "The whole idea of management consulting is that you get to leap-frog your career forward. Instead of getting somewhere in ten years," which for her would be a senior operating role in a company. "You might get there in six years."

The 2008 recession disrupted her journey. Sethi was laid off from her job. Not wanting a large gap on her resume, she sprang into action and quickly found another job, which unfortunately got monotonous and boring. How did she solve that? "I knew that I wanted to do something else, but I didn't know what. So, I decided to take a break." During the 2008 crisis, a career break was imposed on her, and she rebounded with her next job only to find out it wasn't ful-filling. She told me, "This time I took a break consciously to figure out what's next." That break lasted five years. During that time, she got married, had twins, and discovered med-itation and spirituality. With time and a shifting set of life experiences, her goals evolved to be more holistic to include well-being and spiritual growth.

The younger Sethi was not an outlier in being laser focused on her career goals. Recent research from MorningConsult surveyed young Gen Z adults, the generation born between 1997–2012, and found that making money and being success-ful were two universally important life goals, more important than friends, family, or hobbies.

In my experience and observation, a paradox exists in the process of goal setting, in both personal lives and business. A well-written goal is clear and measurable. And yet the moment we put a measurement on it, we limit it. As soon as we set a goal of three times revenue growth in three years, we have limited the possibility to three times (and not ten times). We have also ignored the many other factors that go into a well-run business: employee and customer satisfaction, social responsibility, and so on. In personal life, we focus on professional goals, such as making a million dollars by age thirty. We tend not to include well-being, good health, and relationships. We take them for granted.

Most of our goals are narrow and rigid. This can lead to unexpected disappointments, both in personal life and business.

CONTEMPLATE

1. Have you ever achieved a goal only to find out it didn't make you as happy as you expected? If you could go back in time and revise that goal, how might you rewrite it? Hint: You can expand and add other goals.
2. Which of your current goals might be narrow and rigid? How might you revise them? (We will revisit this contemplation in the next chapter.)

CHAPTER 7

BREAKING THROUGH THE PARADOX OF GOAL SETTING

———

"Almost everything I've written that has survived was written when I didn't try to get anything done."

—NASSIM TALEB

Why does this paradox get created? Is there a way out of it? We'll explore these questions next.

THE GOALS WE DON'T SET

In 2010, the late Clay Christensen, a Harvard Business School professor, wrote an article called, "How Will You Measure Your Life." In the article, Christensen shared an observation. His classmates, like all ambitious people, had set out clear goals for their professional lives. Many went on to achieve those goals and became rich and successful. None of them set out with a goal to commit white collar crime or end up with estranged families. And yet, that is what he found happened with his classmates over and over again.

The problem was not in the goals they set for themselves, but rather the ones they didn't. It didn't occur to them to set goals on being in healthy relationships or living ethical lives. Nothing is inherently wrong in wanting to make millions or attain power. It's just that those goals are myopic. We don't set a goal for being there for our family because we either assume it will be true or don't think of it as a thing requiring an explicit stated goal (although we have probably heard of someone who had a deadbeat dad and set a personal goal to always be there for his own children). This problem lies not just with young people but is an all-too-common tendency in goal setting among all of us. We acquire this tendency toward narrow and rigid goals when we are young and then carry it to all aspects of our lives: parenting, planning a home purchase, even managing the teams and businesses we lead.

Let's expand this discussion from individuals to goals that companies set. After all, companies are led by a collection of individuals who bring the same approach of goal setting to their work. The United States is a capitalist country. As such, profit is considered a noble goal. Shareholder returns are sacred. It is how companies are measured and rewarded, especially by Wall Street. If they don't perform, they are punished with a declining share price or shareholder activism.

Although never stated as a goal, businesses want to endure and last long. Turns out this is hard to achieve. According to data from the Bureau of Labor Statistics, as reported by

Fundera, approximately 20 percent of small businesses fail within the first year. By the end of the second year, 30 percent of businesses will have failed. By the end of the fifth year, about half will have failed. And by the end of the decade, only 30 percent of businesses will remain—a 70 percent failure rate.

In Jim Collins's book, *Built to Last,* the author points to the folly of businesses that focused exclusively on profits and shareholder returns to the detriment of long-term success. He and his partner, Jerry Porras, spent six years studying what they call "visionary companies." Among other factors, these companies had a unique perspective toward profits. The leaders of these companies, he found, understood that profitability is necessary for the organization to exist and fulfill its purpose, but that the company is much more than profits. These leaders pursued both profits and ideology. The book mentions one such leader to illustrate this combination of profit and purpose:

"In 1935, the CEO, Robert W. Johnson Jr., [of Johnson and Johnson] wrote out the company's core ideology in a document called 'Our Credo', which listed the company's responsibilities: first to their customers, second to their employees and so forth. Finally, fifth and last on the list, after all the other responsibilities had been fulfilled, Johnson said that shareholders should receive 'a fair return.'"

Collins's visionary companies were profitable; otherwise they couldn't have sustained growth over a long period of time (they had an average age of 100 years). Their goals, however, were not exclusively focused on profitability. By broadening their goals, they achieved much more than the narrow goal would have yielded.

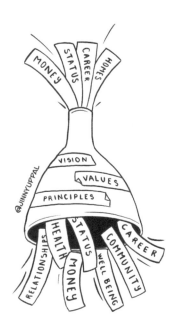

One way to avoid the pitfalls of narrow and rigid goals is to broaden them upfront. If not, perhaps life will do it for you as was in the case of Sethi from the previous chapter. Returning to her story, we last saw her taking a voluntary break during which she built a family and found a spiritual practice. Five years into her break, she decided to get back into corporate life. In prepping her resume, she reached out to a mentor from Booz, her former employer. He made introductions that ultimately led to a senior director of corporate strategy and business development role for a marketing firm. She laughed as she told me, "That's exactly where I wanted to land, after six years in consulting! The added five years gave me experiences and a spiritual perspective on life that most people get when they are in their sixties or when they retire." She had chosen the management consulting route to leapfrog the conventional growth pattern in corporate careers. She narrowly focused her goals on professional success. After being knocked off her journey to her goals once, she embraced the power of pausing to figure out a broader and more holistic set of goals. And in doing so, even though she hadn't intended to, she managed to leapfrog spiritual progress!

THE MOST DIRECT PATH PUSHES THE GOAL AWAY
Setting narrow and rigid goals is not the only problem. Another tendency in goal setting is that we look for the most direct path to achieving them. Ambitious people can be the best and most skilled in setting goals. They then barrel through life with a single-minded pursuit of those goals. Determination, focus, and single-mindedness are considered virtuous qualities. But a direct pursuit of goals can be the very thing that pushes the goal further away. John Kay, a British economist, wrote a treatise on this aspect of approaching goals in his book *Obliquity: Why Our Goals are Best Achieved Indirectly*. While he was writing his book, I was to have my own run-in with this concept.

When I was studying at Harvard Business School (HBS) in 2010, I was assigned an executive coach named Letty Garcia. I approached her for guidance on a topic I had been struggling with. Attending conferences and company events with the goal of networking and making connections had become an important part of my professional life. But there was a problem. I told her, "I hate networking. I don't like going to conferences and meeting people. I never have anything to say; small talk is not my thing. It's all overwhelming and exhausting. And I never make good connections. How can I learn to be better at networking so I can make meaningful contacts?"

Letty started off by giving me a bunch of ideas on my stated goal: better networking and making connections. Her husband was a master networker, and she shared some of his approaches, all of which sounded like more of the same. Then she said something that caught my attention. "You are a very goal-oriented person"—*true words*—"and accomplishment driven." *Agreed.* "If you do something and don't get the results you want, you get frustrated and might want to give up." *Already there.*

She went on. "What if you don't think of networking as a to-do to get something from others, but rather a way of giving something? This way, while you are not sure what will come back, it might be better than you asked for. Plus, you take the pressure off of yourself to meet the goal of 'making connections.'"

What an interesting concept! Her words stayed with me. By the end of my HBS courses, I felt deeply connected with my classmates and was saddened at the thought that I would not see them again. They were spread across the world, and I was not likely to keep up. An idea formed in my head: What if I organized an alumni conference of sorts, not only for my classmates but for all cohorts, here in New York City? This way, everyone, including me, would get to see each other again. We would all expand our network to people from other cohorts. That idea culminated into the first Alumni Summit, a half-day event held in Manhattan in fall 2011. The summit grew to be a wild success. By 2019, the summit had grown into a three-day extravaganza, rotating across major global cities, with tickets selling out in minutes. I chaired the planning committee for four years and stayed on for another two before completely handing it over to later cohorts.

Letty was right. When I took the most direct path of attending networking events to make connections, that goal became elusive and I became frustrated. Changing the approach I took to my goals not only took the pressure off me but also created an event that thousands attended over the years, reconnecting with their classmates as well as beloved professors who always taught a case study or two. While it had never occurred to me to think of setting this as a goal, I now have an accessible alumni network across the world. These are people whom I have reached out to for a variety of discussions and brainstorms over the years, including interviews for this book.

AN INDIRECT PATH TO SUCCESS

I am not suggesting that taking a direct path to results is wrong or ineffective. Companies in Collins's study that exclusively pursued profit have been successful. They just didn't stay as successful for very long. I could have continued to grit my teeth and network in my usual direct style. It's not like I didn't make any connections at all. But it would have continued to generate anxiety, impatience, and disappointment with the results. By broadening my goals and taking an indirect approach to them, I more than exceeded my original goal and created a platform for many to make more meaningful connections with their fellow alumni.

WINNING A FIGHT WITHOUT FIGHTING THE FIGHT

Broadening goals to include noble objectives aside, sometimes it just feels natural to go after a goal with all you've got. That is the case with forest fires. They are harmful. Untold lives and property have been destroyed in forest fires over the decades and centuries. It is natural to set a goal to eliminate or suppress fires and throw everything at it.

Starting in 1910, the National Park Service (NPS) of the United States did just that. They adopted a policy of suppression, which meant controlling fires by fighting them and putting them out. An endless supply of resources was thrown at the problem. It wasn't until 1950, after decades of research and a growing vocal minority, that the NPS woke up to the fact that fighting fires was not only expensive but counter to the ultimate goal of controlling damage from fires. Nature has its own way of house-cleaning to maintain an ecological balance. Interfering with that balance by suppressing all wildfires was causing an unnatural buildup of fuel, leading to more severe breakouts. It also created an unintended side effect: NPS's determined elimination of forest fires had the effect that "some national park areas look more like managed landscapes rather than vestiges of a natural past."

Counterintuitively, research revealed, the best way to fight fires was not to fight them but through selective inaction. Eventually NPS reversed their approach and adopted policies on leaving fires caused by natural events such as lightning alone, thereby acknowledging their overall positive impact on the ecosystem. Moreover, they also adopted a strategy of initiating controlled fires, which helped in house-cleaning to prevent buildup of fuel. When the NPS was bold and ambitious about directly fighting and eliminating fires as a goal, they spent a lot of money without results. Today, NPS's goals and policies are far more comprehensive. Their website acknowledges that "wildland fire will be…allowed to function in its natural ecological role."

Sometimes the better way of achieving a goal is to flip the goal on its head or broaden it to make it more inclusive and purposeful. By giving us a wider base of things we want to accomplish, we won't miss the forest for the trees.

A direct action toward the stated goal can sometimes be counterproductive and push the desired results away. Strategically choosing a counterintuitive approach can yield a nonlinear and less expensive path to the goal.

This is the paradox in goal setting. And yet, awareness of it can be the very tool that helps us master the process of goal setting and create a more efficient, nonlinear path to goals.

CONTEMPLATE

1. Revisit the second contemplation from the previous chapter. What would happen to those goals once you run it through your principles and values filter?
2. Pick a goal that really matters. If you were to take a more indirect and less aggressive path to it, what might that look like?

CHAPTER 8

THE CHANCE EFFECT (OR CAUSE AND EFFECT FALLACY)

"We have, as human beings, a storytelling problem. We're a bit too quick to come up with explanations for things we don't really have an explanation for."

—MALCOM GLADWELL, *BLINK*

THE CROW AND THE COCONUT TREE

Once upon a time, a great coconut tree stood tall, seemingly reaching for the sky. Upon a branch of this tree hung a merry group of coconuts together. As a man on the ground looked up, a crow flew on top of the thick stem that had firmly secured the coconuts to the branch. As if right on cue, the coconuts fell to the ground. The man was amazed. "That crow must have thick claws, look how it dislodged those coconuts! Usually, it takes a man with a sharp knife to cut those loose."

What the man didn't realize was that the coconuts were ripe and ready to fall. The crow landing on that branch at just that moment was a coincidence.

This story is from an ancient Indian text that I've studied called *Yoga Vasiṣṭha*. It illustrates our basic tendency to create cause and effect where none exists. If ancient fables are not your thing, you are in luck. A more modern, eighteenth-century thinker agrees with this fable's insight. Scottish philosopher David Hume famously rejected any logical connection between cause and effect. He believed that all observations of cause and effect were projections of the mind. It is a story the mind makes up. No evidence exists that one thing causes another. All we can say is an event occurred and another one followed

Hume believed that a relationship between cause and effect could not be logically proven. A relationship may exist, it just can't be perceived or proven by humans. The Indian text *Yoga Vasiṣṭha*, on the other hand, completely rejects the existence of cause and effect; it says that all events are random, and it is only the human mind which makes meaning out of events and creates causality between them. My deepest insights on the cause-and-effect fallacy have come from *Yoga Vasiṣṭha*, which happens to align with quantum theory of time. To avoid a tangent in this book, I share those insights in an article titled "Musings on *Yoga Vasiṣṭha*" on my website which will make an interesting read regardless of your own spiritual, scientific, or religious beliefs.

How does this relate to our discussion? It introduces us to one of the root causes of our action bias: overconfidence. While building confidence in ourselves and our ideas is an intrinsic and necessary aspect of growth, the trouble begins when we start creating causality between our actions and outcomes, which is the slippery slope into the land of overconfidence. We start believing in our power to exclusively make something happen. We quickly become overconfident in our own talent, skills, and past choices. If we were successful in the past, we build a virtuous trail of causality between our actions and outcomes, leading to overconfidence in the present.

We routinely underestimate the role of chance in how outcomes are shaped. Sometimes, we look to experts and previous winners for a formula of success; people who themselves routinely downplay the role of luck and randomness and overplay the role of their actions.

Our actions do contribute to the outcome. However, chance has an important, sometimes outsized, role to play. Because we ignore this fact, we think the only or predominant way to get results is through that action. Overconfidence leads to our eventual downfall. And when we get a negative outcome, we are surprised, or we resort to blame. We were so sure our strategy would work! In these scenarios, we fail to understand what really happened, thereby missing out on valuable lessons.

FOOLED BY RANDOMNESS

"There is one world in which I believe the habit of mistaking luck for skill is most prevalent—and most conspicuous—and that is the world of [stock] markets," says Nassim Taleb, a former stock market trader and author.

Taleb wrote a treatise on the subject of cause and effect in his book *Fooled by Randomness,* where he tells stories of traders who were wildly successful. However, it is revealed other macro factors were at play that contributed to their success. They had merely stumbled into the right strategy at the right time. And, when measured over a long enough period of time, that strategy eventually failed. The macro factors changed. But the traders, confident of their secret sauce and unaware of the macro conditions, didn't change their strategies. They were overconfident, and they eventually failed.

Says Taleb, "We often have the mistaken impression that a strategy is an excellent strategy, or an entrepreneur a person endowed with vision or a trader a talented trader, only to realize that 99.9 percent of their past performance is attributable to chance, and chance alone. Ask a profitable investor to explain the reasons for his success; he will offer some deep and convincing interpretation of the results. Frequently, these delusions are intentional and deserve to bear the name 'charlatanism.'"

This insight from an industry insider is alarming. If professionals are at risk of overestimating the probability of success due to overconfidence, what about us mere mortals? Well, I can confirm that the situation is as bad. A research study published in *Journal of Behavioral and Experimental Finance* found that regular investors who are overconfident in their ability to make the right choices are more likely to irrationally buy and sell (they keep taking action), which in turn leads to poor performance. As I look hard for a silver lining here, the only one I can find is that if I am going to be as wrong as the professionals, perhaps I ought to take over my investments and not pay someone else a fee to make mistakes with my money.

Joshing aside, the role of chance applies everywhere. Let's look at the role of luck in business.

THE SECRET OF SUCCESS IN THE TECHNOLOGY ERA: CHANCE

We entered a new era driven by digital technology a few decades ago. Brian Arthur is an economist and is credited with the theory of "increasing returns," which describes the nature of business success in this era. Turns out, Arthur shares Taleb's view on the role of chance in driving success in business.

Arthur points out that most of our current understanding of business and markets came from a previous era, which was characterized by diminishing returns. A hundred years ago, businesses only sold stuff that are physical and tangible: cars, appliances, clothes. These widgets were made from other physical ingredients finite in quantity (commodities like copper, cotton, land, etc.). The size of the market was also finite; only so many adult humans need cars, and populations usually grow at a modest pace. At some point, a given business would become as efficient and scale as much as it could. Thereafter, the returns in that business, and industry, would diminish simply because the supply of physical materials and demand in the form of consumption plateaued.

Today, however, stuff we consume is not always physical. Thanks to technology, we consume ideas, experiences and digital products as much, if not more, than physical products. Seven of the top ten companies in the world are software or technology companies. These companies have no natural limit to how much their returns can increase; they can keep creating newer experiences from imagination combined with bits and bytes in unlimited supply. We have entered an era of, what Arthur calls, increasing returns. Businesses can keep returning more on their original investment if they keep finding the right next idea.

As per Arthur, chance plays an important role in the success of companies in the early days of that industry. "Chance events early in the history of an industry or technology can tilt the competitive balance," he says. "In the real world, if several similar-size firms entered a market at the same time, small, fortuitous events—unexpected orders, chance meetings with buyers, managerial whims—would help determine which ones achieved early sales and, over time, which firm dominated."

"Economic activity is quantified by individual transactions which are too small to quantify, and these small 'random' events can accumulate and become magnified by positive feedback so as to determine the eventual outcome."

If random events determine eventual outcome, then why don't we talk about this huge role that chance plays? Why do we always celebrate visionaries, the heroes and heroines of the business world and their specific actions that led to success? Much like inaction, we can't "see" the events that chance brought about. Individual moments in life are random and too small to quantify. Evidence that chance led to success is hard to come by. People love stories, and they love explanations. Journalists and media, especially, love telling a good story.

When successful people are interviewed, they have a small amount of time during which to succinctly deliver a cause-and-effect story. Short, conclusive soundbites are cool. "These three strategies helped drive our success" sounds better than "We tried a bunch of stuff, but I really don't know how it all came together. We just got lucky." We are the biggest suckers of our own past success story.

THE NEWS THAT EVERYBODY READS

THE NEWS THAT NOBODY READS

The risk in creating a cause-and-effect story is simply this: It reflects the past, infused with luck and other factors that are poorly understood by the protagonist. It is, at best, one way of doing things that happened to work in the past. Entrepreneur and venture capitalist Paul Graham points out, "It can take decades to understand things you thought you understood as they were happening." Time has an interesting way of changing what you were once sure you fully understood.

Until several years ago, I used to congratulate myself on the bold actions I took that led to success. Looking back, I could easily connect the dots on my actions and the results. I made the decision to study abroad. I worked hard and got good grades. I interviewed and got good job offers. Out of the options available to me after graduation, I chose a job in the New York area, a move that set me up for future success. I could list a litany of choices I made and things I did to get where I did. It wasn't until a few years ago that I fully acknowledged the marvelous role of chance events that brought these opportunities to me so I could choose from among them. I happened to come of age at a time when information technology was rising as a whole new industry. I happened to be born into a family where education was encouraged for girls, unlike most of our peer families. Although my parents couldn't afford to fund an American education, I was lucky to get a full scholarship. Two years later, the tech bubble burst and scholarships became hard to come by. Once, my job happened to get outsourced. This event coincided with my wanting to leave the industry I was in: business telecom. The outsourcing landed me in a large global consulting company, where I embarked on a nonlinear path to e-commerce, which was in the early stages as a new industry. My career grew rapidly along with that industry.

Did my actions take me to the right people and opportunities, or did accidental coincidences lead me to where they were? What was the cause, and what was the effect here? I don't know. Frankly, it doesn't matter. What I do know is that luck played a huge role. And whatever I did in the past may or may not work in the future. So, I should stay open to possibilities outside of any formula my mind can make up from past success.

I am not dismissing the role of action in achieving success. I invite you to not dismiss the often-outsized role of chance either.

Does this mean we stop acting and let chance do its thing? No. The point is not to become overconfident that we know exactly what to do when faced with a situation. The point is also to avoid regret if we fail. Regret implies I or someone else could have done something better or different. It's a simplistic assumption that things happened because of what I or someone else did.

The point is to give up on those stories.

How about we just study luck and randomness and make that our strategy? If that were possible, then the decades of research on gambling would by now have given us techniques to guarantee future wins. The problem with studying randomness is that any such endeavor will naturally reflect on the past, which itself is a unique chance collection of events that may not repeat in the future.

The call to action (!) here is to reduce the obsessive focus on our formulaic doing and acknowledge that life is a dynamic process, ever changing and ever new. Being in observation and incrementally building a nonlinear action plan can get us "there" faster than any past set of actions that worked back then. Becoming aware of our tendency of overconfidence has an interesting side effect: It opens us up to newer possibilities.

We take in new information more willingly. Inspired thought shows up. And when we act on inspired thought, what we get is inspired action. We flow with life.

CONTEMPLATION

1. Revisit a past success, and rethink the role chance may have played.
2. Revisit a current plan of action and consider: If chance truly plays an outsized role in life, how might your plan change? Hint: You might want to pause and take stock of new information more often.

AN INTRODUCTION TO PART 3

———

Thus far, we have seen the major causes of action bias and obstacles that get in the way of Mastering Action. To some extent, awareness of these behavioral traits can help us get past them. In the stories of the people we met, they shared their own recipes for overcoming their action bias.

This book is not about slowing down; it is about getting results and driving progress toward what we want in life. Inaction has two sides. One where we are helpless in the face of our fears; we are frozen into inaction. The other, what this book is about, is thoughtfully making a choice to not act or to take a different course of action than the norm suggests. It is an empowering use of inaction.

By now, we know a lot more about the direct and indirect triggers of our action bias through stories and research. We learned from the protagonists of our stories how they learned to manage their susceptibility to their action bias.

DIRECT TRIGGERS OF ACTION BIAS :

ACTING WITHOUT THINKING

REGRET OFF LOSS

OVERCONFIDENCE

INDIRECT TRIGGERS OF ACTION BIAS:

NARROW AND RIGID GOALS

DEFAULTING TO AN ACTION PLAYBOOK

CREATING FALSE CAUSALITY

@JINNYUPPAL

The next part deals with techniques which may sound counterintuitive but actually directly help create a space for creative ideas to make themselves known to us. They help preempt the action bias and lead us to inspired action. You may find that these techniques, such as mind-wandering, daydreaming, laziness, and procrastination have a strong negative stigma attached to them. A major reason is they are usually associated with a lack of control over our lives; they usually imply a sort of helplessness. But when leveraged as a thoughtful choice, the same behaviors can do wonders in driving creative thinking and progress. This book is not about inaction for the sake of it; rather, it is about nonlinear paths to getting great results. So, let's get to it!

PART 3

DEVELOPING A PRACTICE OF MASTERING ACTION

CHAPTER 9

THE POWER OF SILENCE

"Silence can have meaning. Like the zero in mathematics, it is an absence with a function."

—WILLIAM J. SAMARIN, *LANGUAGE OF SILENCE*

In the United States and many other western countries, talking is often considered a sign of engagement. Young people and early career employees are often taught to say something to be a part of the conversation. In many colleges, a portion of the grade goes to class participation. And yet, by the time we become adults, we overuse this training and start using talking as an exclusive tool to communicate and be understood. *Silence, on the other hand, is a powerful tool to understand.*

If used correctly, it can, at one end of the benefit scale, help us understand the situation more deeply so we can respond rather than react. At the other end, it can help tilt the balance of power toward us, whether in personal or business relationships.

WHEN EVERYONE IS TALKING,
NO ONE IS LISTENING

This chapter is about strategic and not helpless silence. It's not about looking the other way or allowing yourself to become a victim. There are specific moments in life, where the default reaction may be to speak, but a thoughtful silence could get better results than any amount of talking would. We will visit a few.

SILENCE IN DEBATE AND DISAGREEMENT

"Jinny, what is going on with you and Wang? You seem to not be getting along," my manager said.

I was taken aback and then mortified. In an email exchange the previous day, I had proposed a new idea to my team of peers. Wang, one of many the email was sent to, replied to everyone, pointing out flaws in the idea. I felt his email had undermined me and would influence others to disagree. Irritated, I had replied privately and accused him of being uncooperative and difficult. Clearly my language and tone offended him, prompting him to tell our mutual manager who now wanted to know what was going on. I did not know my manager knew about it and was caught unaware by the question. This incident occurred two or three years out of grad school. I scrambled together an explanation while sitting in my manager's office. I don't remember being very gracious about the entire incident. But I did learn a good lesson on not emailing while upset.

In a disagreement, it is very tempting to argue with each point, tear it apart, and undermine the other party—all in order to prove why you are right. That approach can quickly become a dog fight, and all parties can get bruised no matter who wins.

One solution is to stay silent on a specific point that is hard to argue or not worth fighting over. Sometimes it is better to wait for a better opportunity, which may come up sooner than expected. If I had been living in the United States in the '80s, I could have learned this lesson from an iconic debate moment between Senator Lloyd Bensten and Senator Dan Quayle, both running for vice president in the 1988 US presidential elections.

Senator Quayle, in this debate moment widely available online, addressed criticism of being too young to be VP by comparing himself with Jack Kennedy who had been president of the United States at a young age. He argued that he had the experience, even if he didn't have the years. When he was finished, Senator Bensten paused for a couple of seconds and then said, "Senator, I served with Jack Kennedy. I knew

Jack Kennedy; Jack Kennedy was a friend of mine. Senator, you are no Jack Kennedy."

On the one hand, Quayle had a good defense to the age criticism, which was then being used against him. By being silent on this defense of his age, which was tough to refute, Bensten, his much older adversary, chose a tangential argument to make. Kennedy was a known and loved figure, a proven politician. No one would disagree with Bensten's argument ("You are no Jack Kennedy"). In fact, he damned Quayle by implying he was way out of his depth comparing himself with the great Jack Kennedy. Oddly, his tangential argument made Quayle seem not mature enough, indirectly making the point that Quayle was too young.

"If You Can't Say Anything Nice, Don't Say Anything at All"

—MARGARET ATWOOD

The quote above is a nice saying that very few actually follow in real life. The fact is that insults and rudeness are more common than we would like. Social media has become a mouthpiece for people to publicly air grievances and criticism with impunity, from the safe confines of their home or office. Handling criticism is one of the greatest leadership skills. I can't think of a better example of how to use silence while handling an insult than the story of Steve Jobs.

In 1997, Steve Jobs had recently returned to lead Apple as CEO, about ten years after he had been ousted. He was killing old ideas in the company and bringing in new ones. In an audience Q&A at one of his talks, someone had this to say: "It's sad and clear that on several counts you've discussed, you don't know what you're talking about." The person then went on to challenge Jobs's choice of specific technologies that he was betting on. This person then demanded an explanation. "And when you're finished with that, perhaps you can tell us what you personally have been doing for the last seven years."

What might you do in the face of a direct assault such as this? Jobs paused for ten seconds. He looked down. He took a drink of water. Then he spoke a few words. He seemed unable to finish the sentence. Then he paused again, for another eight seconds. If you watch the video, freely available online, it feels as if even though he is silent, the wheels are turning in his head.

When he does speak, what follows is a case study of how to respond to an insult of that kind. He starts off by acknowledging the truth in the person's challenge. "One of the hardest things when you are trying to affect change is that people like this gentleman are right!" He then stressed a qualifier, "*...in some areas.*" Then he lifted the audience into the much broader and grander vision he had for Apple. He shared his vision of starting out with the customer needs and building products for those needs rather than starting with the available technology and force feeding the customer. He shared his goal of selling eight or ten billion dollars' worth of product a year. He acknowledged the person again and said that mistakes would be made on the way to this grand vision, preempting future criticism bound to come his way. He ignored the question about his past activity.

It is quite an experience to watch his use of silence: looking down, not making eye contact with the audience, drinking water, all of which helped him disengage and refocus away from the direct question and back to his own vision. He answered a question about his future vision that no one asked.

Jobs went on to bring his vision to life over the next few decades and established Apple as a pioneer in design-inspired products. A short silence is sometimes all it takes to respond and not react.

When we talk, we usually aim to convince. Not talking, listening, or short pauses in between dialogue help take in what the other person said and resist the urge to react or persuade right away. Jobs could have launched into a defense of his past actions and his new ideas. By giving himself space of a few seconds, he reconnected with his own vision and spoke from there. Counterintuitively enough, the stronger the disagreement or debate, the more silence helps.

SILENCE IN NEGOTIATIONS

Another situation where silence can be powerful is negotiations. While the temptation during negotiations is to outguess all the moves our opponent might make, the use of silence can be a powerful tool to get concessions, or at least incrementally elicit useful information from the other party.

In the movie *The Godfather*, a scene shows the godfather Vito Corleone being approached by a landlord who had previously evicted a woman. The landlord had found out that the woman was a friend of the great Don Corleone's wife. In this classic scene, the landlord approaches Don Corleone to make peace and offer to give the apartment back to the woman. Upon listening to what seems a fair deal, Don Corleone stays silent. The landlord, feeling pressured by the silence, sweetens the offer; he will allow the woman to keep her dog. The don still doesn't speak. The blabbering landlord then offers to reduce her rent. Now the don speaks and thanks the landlord, signaling an end to the discussion. By leveraging the power of silence, the don extracts more concessions than he might have had he spoken or used threats.

One might dismiss this story because we are talking about *The Godfather*. The landlord is clearly intimidated by the reputation of the don; it is no surprise that the don got the better of the bargain. What if you are the weaker party and want a concession from someone more powerful? Could you use silence without damning yourself?

One such story is that of Richard Pound, a Canadian lawyer by training. For several decades he has represented the International Olympic Committee (IOC) in various roles, spanning television and sponsorship negotiations, among others. In the 1980s, the IOC came up with the Olympic Program, which solicited sponsorship from global businesses such as credit card and beverages companies. In this program, the sponsor would fund the IOC and in turn be able to use "official sponsor of the Olympics" in their marketing campaigns. Corporate sponsorships for sports and other mega events are routine now, but they were a new idea for the Olympics back then.

In the early days, this was a hard idea to sell. The potential return of such a sponsorship was difficult to quantify and predict. The IOC approached American Express, then and now a leading provider of financial services across the globe. American Express turned them down. They then went to Visa next, who agreed. A sponsorship between Visa and the IOC was announced sometime in 1983 to 1984.

As the marketing campaigns from Visa picked up, Pound and his team noticed something. He told me, "They [American Express] instigated a series of ambush marketing campaigns against Visa," referring to a marketing strategy whereby a brand tries to associate themselves with a major event even though they are not an official partner. They were riding someone else's marketing wave without paying for it.

Why would they do that? "I think they realized that they had missed a huge opportunity and a worldwide platform. They wanted to get on the Olympic bandwagon even though they had missed it," said Pound. Over the subsequent years, the IOC litigated and sued American Express for multiple instances of ambush marketing. But litigating is time consuming and expensive—especially against someone with deep pockets like American Express.

When Atlanta won the rights to host the Olympics in 1996, Pound realized that since the CEO of American Express lived in Atlanta, they wouldn't let such a chance go by without ambushing it in a big way. Pound asked for a meeting with their CEO, Jim Robinson. He agreed.

In the meeting, Pound reasoned that what American Express had been doing was unfair. He argued they had approached American Express first and had been turned down. He asked that they stop co-opting the Visa Olympics marketing campaign. Robinson defended his company's practices. He said the marketing was working wonderfully for them and he had no reason to stop.

Pound then played his final card and said to the CEO, "The first time I see anything that looks like ambush marketing, I am going to call a press conference. I am going to invite the US women's gymnastics team, who are going to share how Visa has been helping them, not American Express. And then I am going to reach into my pocket, take out my American Express card, and cut it in front of the cameras. And I am going to say that I don't want to do business with a company with this kind of ethics." Then, Pound stopped talking.

In the 1990s, before social media, viral news, or the "woke" and "corporate responsibility" movements, such a grand gesture may or may not have worked. Robinson was clearly in a great position of power, and Pound knew it. Robinson could have said, "Fine, go for it."

What followed Pound's declaration was silence. That silence lasted three minutes. Imagine being the only person in a room with the head of one of the most powerful companies in the world. Imagine the seconds and minutes ticking by. Pound waited and kept waiting.

Finally, Robinson spoke. He acknowledged they had indeed turned down the opportunity to sponsor the Olympics. He would stop all ambush marketing. Pound stood up and thanked him. Mission accomplished; he left.

These examples happen to be about confrontational negotiations with a win–lose outcome. But all negotiations benefit from a strategic use of silence. A 2020 research paper entitled, "Silence Is Golden: Extended Silence, Deliberative Mindset, and Value Creation in Negotiation," showed that, in fact, silence of a few seconds reduces the fixed-pie mindset in negotiations and leads to value creation. In other words, introducing deliberate pauses of a few seconds can lead the negotiating parties to come up with ideas that expand the pie being split, benefiting both parties.

SILENCE IN TEAM MEETINGS

Conflict or confrontation isn't the only time when silence is useful. It is a powerful tool to improve our understanding of the situation. Team meetings are one situation where silence can help improve productivity for everyone. The technology company Amazon is known for pioneering their silent meeting approach. Their CEO, Jeff Bezos, has been quoted as saying, "This is the smartest thing we ever did at Amazon." In this approach, all attendees sit quietly reading from the same six-page memo that has previously been circulated. This quiet time gives everyone time to develop a common understanding of the idea before getting into a discussion.

This practice is now increasingly used in other companies. Pierre-Yves Picau, a software engineer, wrote about his experience at Square, a major technology company: "The first time I went through such a meeting, it felt a little bit odd, but I quickly realized how much more we were getting done in the same amount of time [as in a traditional meeting]."

The idea is equally powerful in all forms of communication and not just meetings. Visionaries and well-known leaders such as Jack Dorsey, Elon Musk, and Tim Cook are known to use silence lasting several seconds when speaking or when they are asked a question. They are not playing mind games; they are collecting their thoughts seeking to understand before responding. The next chapter references neuroscience research demonstrating that the mind connects dots meaningfully when it is not focused on a task. Talking is a task that focuses our attention outward; silence takes our attention inward and allows time to connect those dots. It allows us to align with aspirations, beliefs, values, purpose, and goals. A pause lasting only a few seconds in the middle of a conversation can be enough to see the situation very differently than if you rushed by talking through it.

Tech era companies are not unique in benefiting from silence in meetings. Quoting a collection of research, a 2019 *Harvard Business Review* article presents silence as an effective technique to remove root causes of ineffective decision-making in meetings. As an example, people are often intimidated by the presence of senior leaders, which holds them back from speaking up. If silence is thoughtfully employed, it can help junior people contribute ideas that may otherwise go unheard.

SILENCE TO SAVE YOURSELF

Like most behaviors in this part of the book, it is possible to misuse silence or become a victim of it. In the story of *The Godfather*, the don clearly uses silence to intimidate. Most of us have experienced the silent death stare from an angry parent, which inflicted more fear than any number of verbal threats. While interviewing for this book, I heard a story of silence being used to successfully intimidate a colleague. I came across stories of how, during a cross examination in the court of law, witnesses damned themselves through unnecessary admissions and confessions in their eagerness to talk to fill an awkward gap in conversation.

HOW TO TALK YOURSELF
INTO A GUILTY VERDICT

I almost damned myself once. I had been issued a ticket for a parking violation. I felt quite adamant that the signs were not very clear and there weren't enough of them. I got it into my head to plead not guilty and got a court appointment to appear in person. While I was standing in front of the judge, I tried to follow the exchange of conversation between him and the prosecutor. The judge seemed to be questioning the prosecutor on the ticket. In a silent gap when they both seemed to be thinking, I interjected, overzealous, to make my case: "May I explain what happened?" The prosecutor turned to me and said, "No. Don't say anything." Thankfully, I took the hint. Turned out there was a technical mistake on the ticket, which caused the case to be dismissed. Had I barged ahead with a defense, I might have confused the matter, possibly confirming my guilt. After all, I did park unlawfully, regardless of my personal complaints on the signs.

As much as this chapter is about using silence to understand the situation before responding, it is also about developing an ability to tolerate it so we are not used by someone else deploying this tool. In a situation of trust, both parties are likely to benefit from silence. In the absence of trust when silence is being used to intimidate or gain a one-sided advantage, developing a comfort with silence can help us reduce our disadvantage. Or perhaps even turn it around to an advantage!

Mastering action is knowing when to act and when not to act; it is allowing inspired action to come through. In a conversation, talking is the action and silence is inaction. Silence helps arrest the tendency toward hasty action while speaking. Being okay with silence builds confidence in thoughtfully staying inactive. It helps build a capability of observation, which in turn can reveal better information we can then act upon.

We have seen several examples of leveraging the power of silence in life. This is not meant to be a compilation of all possible techniques of using silence. Silence is something to be allowed, not summoned or forced. Whichever illustration in this chapter suits you, allow it in, rather than go work on it. It is important not to start chasing silence either!

In the next chapter, we will explore another atypical exercise to drive creative progress: mind-wandering and daydreaming.

CONTEMPLATION

1. What about silence of several seconds in a conversation is appealing or intimidating to you? Assume this is with a person you don't have an intimate relationship with.
2. Think back to a conversation where the other person unexpectedly fell silent for an unusually long time. What did you feel? How did it feel in your body?

CHAPTER 10

DAYDREAMING AND MIND-WANDERING AS CREATIVE TOOLS

———

"I live my daydreams in music."

—ALBERT EINSTEIN

As part of researching this book's thesis, I became curious about the impact of activity versus inactivity on the brain. So, I went to work on my favorite search engine. I was expecting to find something along the lines of meditation. Imagine my surprise when I came across a series of neuroscience research articles pointing to daydreaming and mind-wandering as powerful mental constructs that aid creative thinking, boost productivity, and even improve goal setting. As a long-term practitioner of meditation, I am familiar with the common narrative of a wandering/distracted mind as a bad thing and meditation as the antidote. Here was research challenging that notion. I am not talking about background thinking while running errands. This is spacing out, wool gathering, staring into nothing—kind of free-roaming castle building.

I have long been aware of my own mind's tendency to wander and daydream. As a practitioner of meditation, I would try to intercept my distracted mind when I became aware of it. Sometime in 2020, I had made an observation while pondering over my daydreaming tendency over the years. I realized my daydreams had a recurring pattern. I would dream a broad narrative over and over, with changes in the scene setting. The narrative usually reflected something I wanted, something that made me happy in the dream but wasn't true in real life. For example, in a new role where I was still finding ways to integrate with the team, my daydreams would be about just that: my colleagues and I having a good time, laughing, and making jokes. After a few weeks or months, I would integrate with the team, and that particular collection of daydreams would go away. This would then be replaced with the next set of daydreams months or even years later, representing the next situation in my life. I am an introvert. I tend to think inwardly more than talk outwardly when facing an issue or a problem. I remember wondering back then, could it be that daydreaming was my mind's way of bringing my attention to an unfulfilled, perhaps even unexpressed, wish? Was my subconscious leaking my most cherished desire to the surface, asking me to pay attention?

Here was research finally answering my question. "Daydreaming typically represents a kind of mental rehearsal, maintaining the brain in a state of readiness to respond," says Josie Glausiusz, who wrote a paper in *Psychology Today* on daydreaming. It was as if I was exploring and practicing pathways in my daydreams to eventually play it out in real life. Once the daydream had served its purpose, it went away.

Mind-wandering is a less choreographed, more free-form type of daydreaming. It is the mind that flits from one topic to another with no apparent purpose or narrative. Turns out mind-wandering also has an advantageous impact on creative thinking.

MIND-WANDERING YOUR WAY TO A CLIENT DEAL

Herre van Kaam is an entrepreneur and a Dutch native. He is the co-owner of a consultancy that advises health care businesses on transformation and innovation. Pitching to clients for new business is part and parcel of his life; it's where the rubber meets the road. He accidentally discovered mind-wandering as a technique back in 2012. This technique now forms a part of his and his team's approach to work.

Van Kaam was scheduled to make a pitch to the board of a potential client along with three other team members. The meeting was at the client site. They were to be the first of three competing teams making the pitch. The meeting was in Kampen, Netherlands, a two-hour train ride from his hometown. Because of the train schedules, he arrived an hour early and decided to go for a walk and take in the new city. He didn't practice or rehearse the pitch. He just walked around letting his mind wander.

By the time he got to the meeting, he was relaxed and feeling good. As was typical, the meeting opened with everyone sitting around the table, clients on one side, pitching team on the other. After introductions were over, van Kaam noticed the coffee pot was empty. He got up to make himself coffee and asked others if they wanted some. A few took him up on his offer. Normally, he would be tense in a client meeting, deliver a rehearsed pitch, and limit his interaction to answering questions from the client. A consultant getting up to make coffee for everyone, including the host, was unusual behavior. The pitch was on how to encourage autonomy among the rank and file of that organization. He wanted to demonstrate what that might look like, so he took up the "job" of making much-needed coffee for everyone instead of waiting for the host to do so. In the meeting, instead of rushing into answers, he chose to answer many of the questions with additional clarifying questions. In engaging with him, the clients started answering their own queries. He would then wrap up the discussion with a summary. He thought the walk relaxed him and influenced his way of engaging with others in the meeting.

Van Kaam's team didn't win the pitch. But the board of the client team asked if he would consider joining the winning team. They didn't want his team; they wanted him. This was a highly unusual suggestion. He was part of an ad hoc team of individual consultants who had been put together to make the pitch. While he was a free agent, he didn't think it appropriate to jump ship. He floated the client's suggestion to his current team as well the winning team. They all agreed van Kaam should join the team who won, which he did.

Taking a walk and doing nothing is now part of his meeting prep. He doesn't mentally rehearse or prep during these walks. He lets his mind wander between things going on at home or work. Of course, a walk is not always possible. "Sometimes I don't have time. And I always regret it." He has an interesting way of describing his experience of a meeting when he is relaxed versus not.

"When I am relaxed [in a meeting], I feel like we are sitting at a roundtable. Everyone is in their chair. But I can virtually sit in their chair. I can feel what they are feeling. I can guess what they are going to say. When I am not relaxed, I feel like I am in the center of the meeting, as if I am in the eye of the hurricane. I become attached to what I am saying, not what others are saying. It becomes about me against them. Sometimes these meetings get tense. And [if I am also tense] I can no longer take control of the meeting. I only know this is happening because my body constricts and my heart rate jumps. I know it's happening because my body tells me that; my mind doesn't tell me that."

What does he do when that happens? "I call it out. I say that something is wrong in the way we are discussing and that it doesn't feel good. Maybe we should take a break. When I say it out loud, others usually acknowledge it. Everyone can feel the tension, but someone has to call it out." Being relaxed makes him more connected and empathetic to everyone else in the meeting. Taking a walk and allowing his mind to wander before critical meetings allows him to be more relaxed.

Van Kaam's wife is a friend of mine and describes him as someone who is "very good at doing nothing." I had previously read about a Dutch concept called "niksen," which sounded similar to how his wife described him. I asked van Kaam about it.

"Niksen is a funny word. It's a verb, which means doing nothing. It's as if you are doing something but that something is nothing. When someone asks, 'What are you doing this afternoon?' I say, 'Ik ga niksen,' which means I don't have any plans. And I don't want to make any plans." He laughed as he said, "It makes it clear that you are not invited to my plans of doing nothing."

I was reminded of a word that was part of my vocabulary growing up: "timepass." It is a slang in Mumbai indicating hanging around doing nothing of consequence. It would go something like this. A friend calls, "What are you doing today?" Me: "Nothing, just doing timepass."

By the time I grew up, timepass had become a thing of the past. Hanging around doing nothing, especially when there was a laundry list of things to do, often led to a guilt trip. Turns out I am not alone in feeling the guilt.

Even though he knows a walk helps him engage much better in meetings, van Kaam also experiences feelings of guilt. "I always felt guilty about walking in the park for an hour before a meeting. My co-owner used to ask me, 'Herre, you are taking a walk in the park. Who are you billing that to?' But I felt like I needed to do that; it's part of how I work. I told my co-owner I would take a walk on my own time. But now I notice others are starting to do it. It's becoming a habit in my company. We have also switched to fee-based billing away from hourly billing."

Whether we call it mind-wandering, timepass, or niksen, neuroscience research explains how and why these non-activities can often lead to creative and breakthrough ideas.

THE BRAIN'S DEFAULT MODE NETWORK

Our understanding of our brain made a major leap forward in 1998 when American neurologist Marcus Raichle wrote his seminal paper on the Default Mode Network (DMN). He and his colleagues had observed that when the mind doesn't have anything to do, it starts processing everything it knows from the past and starts planning the future. It starts to make sense of it all. Certain parts of the brain come alive when this activity (or non-activity!) is going on. The DMN is different from those parts of the brain that come alive when we are focused on a task.

To understand this more in depth, I reached out to Mary Helen Immordino-Yang, professor and brain researcher at the University of California, Los Angeles (UCLA). She explained to me, "When we are engaging with a task, we are taking in information; we are not generally making deep meaning out of it. It is our ability to decouple from the outside world that allows us to make rich, ethical meaning out of life." As I understood her, when the DMN is active, the brain starts considering our values, life purpose, ethics, morals, and so on and applies it to the data we previously took in through our senses.

As Raichle puts it, "The brain is in the prediction business." When it's taking in sensory information, it starts processing it. When it is doing nothing, it is connecting the dots, planning, and building a future. In an editorial piece for a University of California, Berkeley publication called "How Mind-Wandering May Be Good for You," writer and former psychologist Jill Suttie points out a collection of research indicating that mind-wandering can help with job performance and goal setting among other things. If the mind is allowed to roam freely, the chances of a creative insight, the "aha moment," are higher than when we are focused on something all the time.

Come to think of it, this should come as no surprise. Think Archimedes and Newton, connecting the dots toward their major discoveries while chilling out in a bathtub or under the apple tree. Many people talk of getting their best ideas in the shower or while driving. While spontaneous mind-wandering is a great source of ideas, could we strategically harness this capability?

While writing this book, I decided to experiment and allow mind-wandering instead of intercepting it. It wasn't easy. A couple of minutes in, I would automatically pick up the phone to check news feeds or play music. Soon, it became more natural. Tiny idea bombs would burst forth; even sentences and phrases for this book would show up, which I would then develop later on. Months later, I had forgotten all about this experiment, and life got busy. Finishing the manuscript became a deadline-driven activity. During my final weeks of writing the manuscript, I recreated my calendar to make sure I was balancing my time well. I remembered the abandoned mind-wandering experiment. I added what seemed like a weird entry into my calendar: thirty minutes of mind-wandering twice a week. The idea was not to sit and mind-wander at that exact time, but to serve as a reminder to deliberately make time for it. Even a twenty-minute period of staring out the window, doing nothing, would help me remember all sorts of research and interesting ideas I had accumulated months earlier.

When I first read this research, I was deeply committed to the idea that mind-wandering and daydreaming are negative mental behaviors. It took me months to fully accept it as a positive behavior, when harnessed correctly. It was interesting for me to notice this particular chapter—between its first version, when I had just begun my research, and the second, which I wrote after giving mind-wandering a fair try—had transformed and became much more robust and complete. I myself could connect the dots between what I was learning much better.

MIND-WANDERING AS A CHOICE

All this comes with a caveat. If the daydreaming and mind-wandering is uncontrolled or filled with obsessive, negative thoughts, then it becomes detrimental to daily functioning. Those struggling with attention deficit hyper-activity disorder (ADHD) find it hard to stay focused in their day-to-day tasks. That's when you are not mind-wandering; the mind is wandering you. The key is to harness this power-ful capability of the brain rather than get carried away with it.

For most of us, living grown-up adult lives filled with careers, families, and other worldly responsibilities, the problem is not too much but too little daydreaming and mind-wan-dering. The key is to be aware of the content of our day-dreams and harvest them for meaningful thoughts and ideas. Everyone has an aspiration, whether it is to make millions of dollars or serve the underprivileged. Mind-wandering can reveal hidden, nonlinear pathways to our goals in a way that no amount of focused work will. It's the combination of aspi-rations and free roaming castle building during mind-wan-dering that ultimately helps us plot and create a future in accordance with, you guessed it, our dreams.

MIND-WANDERING VS. MEDITATION: AND THE WINNER IS...YOU!

All this research created a conflict between my understand-ing of meditation and mind-wandering. Meditation teach-ers routinely give the example of the monkey mind, which keeps jumping from the past to the future, never staying in the present. Meditation is then presented as the antidote to the monkey mind. Research proves that mindful med-itation can aid in creative thinking. Research also proves that mind-wandering can drive creative ideas. To top it all, research proves these two are opposing mental phenomena. You can't "do" both at the same time.

What gives?

Psychologist Jonathan Schooler conducted a study to compare mindfulness, a Buddhist meditation technique, and mind-wandering to answer precisely this question. He concluded that they are different pathways to the same outcome: improved creativity. Mind-wandering is more likely to yield sudden creative insights, as if the idea came to you out of thin air. Mindfulness, specifically the practice of being focused on something like the breath, leads to creative problem-solving through improved analytical ability, which is being able to observe deeply and systematically arrive at the solution as if you found it deep down there.

Schooler found that a "greater tendency toward mind-wandering increased problem-solving when…approached in an insightful way, but impaired problem-solving when… approached in an analytic way. Greater mindfulness was consistently associated with increased problem-solving performance when…approached with analytic strategy."

Sometimes research papers can get nuanced and dense. The way I interpret these findings is that it's to-mae-to versus to-mah-to. They are both about practicing non-doing and lead to creative solutions that frenzied doing won't lead to. Mind-wandering, when not excessive, isn't the villain. Mindfulness or meditation isn't the only road to creativity. They each have a role to play. Mind-wandering comes more naturally to most of us; meditation takes training.

THE MANY WAYS OF DRIVING
CREATIVE THOUGHT

Mind-wandering, daydreaming, meditation, even nature walking are all great tools to have in our toolkit. They increase awareness of the self and the mind and what we truly want. They all unveil ideas and thoughts that can lead to inspired action far more than any amount of hard work can. As Buddhist teacher Nhat Hanh said, "Often we tell ourselves, don't just sit there, do something! But when we practice awareness, we discover that the opposite may be more helpful: Don't just do something, sit there!"

EXTROVERSION VS. INTROVERSION

All this left one final question on my mind. As an introvert, I gain energy when I withdraw from the world. After I got past my initial resistance to these concepts, mind-wandering, daydreaming, and meditation became relatively easy for me to embrace. How about extroverts who gain energy when they engage with the world and people? How about people who love being active and can't really sit still? Are they doomed to not getting the benefits of these techniques?

I turned, once again, to UCLA researcher Immordino-Yang, whom we met earlier. "There's going to be differences in what people find restorative. Some people like to work in the garden, go for a walk, sweep the kitchen, or do something that keeps their hands moving and their mind a little bit occupied in an automatic way. They need some activity that uses up that physical energy but doesn't use up your full mental space. It's not the case that in order to be reflecting you need to be sitting still."

The problem occurs when we don't allow ourselves enough of both states, active and restorative. "It's really about being adaptive, having the flexibility of moving between the states. That's what we need to cultivate," she continued.

Inserting restorative moments throughout the day is a great way to allow creative insights. Whether you are an extrovert or introvert, it's worthwhile giving mind-wandering a try. You can start small. After speaking with van Kaam, I started inserting ten minutes of mind-wandering before my most critical meetings. Regardless of the ultimate outcome of the meeting, I enjoy these conversations far more than I used to. That alone is worth the ten minutes!

If you are busy and can't find the time, then to you I quote health and wellness author Sukhraj Dhillon with my modification in brackets: "You should sit in meditation [or mind-wandering] for twenty minutes every day—unless you're too busy; then you should sit for an hour."

This chapter visited tools which are usually scorned but, if used wisely, can help drive creative problem solving. While we are in the mood to discover contrarian paths to progress, let's visit a couple more next.

CONTEMPLATION

1. Children often daydream and space out. You probably did that when you were a child. When did you stop?
2. When you see an adult sitting in public, seemingly spaced out, what do you really think of them?

CHAPTER 11

BEING LAZY AND PROCRASTINATING YOUR WAY TO RESULTS

"Anyone who is both clever and lazy is qualified for the highest leadership duties, because he possesses the mental clarity and strength of nerve necessary for difficult decisions."

—KURT VON HAMMERSTEIN-EQUORD

"Kabir, I am telling you for the last time, PICK UP YOUR LEGOS, otherwise no ice cream for you!" This is followed by five-year-old Kabir scrambling into action, picking up a few pieces. And as soon as Mom is out of sight, he slips back into whatever he wants to do—play, talk to himself, or something else.

This is a common conversation in the house of Divya Kaur, a millennial mom who lives in the United States. You can replace "no ice cream" with "you can't go biking" or some other threat. She and her husband have busy jobs, two boys under six, and a full social life. Kaur is also an avid chef who loves to make things from scratch, including biscotti and mozzarella. And she loves doing creative projects with her children such as making a playhouse together.

I asked Kaur what her goal was in trying to get her kids to do their chores. "Honestly, in the short term, it's self-preservation," she said. "If they don't pick up after themselves, I will have to. Long term, I want them to have ownership of their lives. I want them to learn to be independent."

I thought it was interesting that she hadn't said anything about teaching them responsibility. I asked her about it. "I think of responsibility as something you have to do. Whereas I want to teach them to be empowered. To learn how they can take care of their lives and things."

Throughout my own adolescence (I am Gen X), I was told by my mother, "Do your studies now, and when you grow up, you can do whatever you want." It was a promise of freedom in the future if I learned to focus on the right priorities, in this context, my education.

Each generation and geography of parents pass on values and ethics that are important to them. For many Americans, the work ethic passed down by their parents is that hard work pays off. Anyone can be successful if they work hard at it. Regardless of geography though, as children and young adults, we are taught the importance of prioritizing certain kinds of tasks over others. As we grow older, the narrative changes to, "You need to work hard to be successful and get what you want." Hard work becomes synonymous with doing. Hard work also becomes the opposite of being lazy and procrastinating, which are labeled negative qualities. Nike's "*Just Do It*" has become a mantra for our times. You can find any number of tools and self-help guides on how to stop procrastinating or being lazy.

While serial procrastination and helpless laziness can indeed get in the way of progress, the very same behaviors can be harnessed to lead us to productive and just-in-time action and away from chasing action.

ACTIVE VS. PASSIVE PROCRASTINATION

Procrastination is not always a bad thing. The Warby Parker founders, whom we met in chapter 5, outwardly seemed to be procrastinating with their idea for an online business. But in reality, they were using that time to study user behaviors and ways to make it easier to order spectacles, the product they wanted to sell, online. Even though others started selling spectacles online before them, they were perfecting the process and customer experience. Today, Warby Parker owns the online eyeglasses category.

This experience got Adam Grant, the professor who declined to invest in them, intrigued enough that he made a study of procrastination for his book, *Originals: How Non-Conformists Move the World*. He found that choosing to procrastinate was one of the habits of these originals. In his research, Grant found that "[people] who rush in and do everything early are rated as less creative than people who procrastinate moderately." Grant says, "Procrastination gives you time to consider divergent ideas, to think in *nonlinear ways, to make unexpected leaps*" (italics are mine). He is talking about people who choose to procrastinate—not the habitual and helpless procrastinators.

Researchers Angela Hsin Chun Chu and Jin Nam Choi have also studied this behavioral trait and distinguish between "passive" and "active" procrastinators. Passive procrastinators are those who can't help it. They procrastinate because they are paralyzed with indecision, unable to focus, perhaps depressed or unmotivated. They are unable or unwilling to face the reality of the underlying dissonance between the task and their emotions about it.

Active procrastinators, on the other hand, choose to delay. They either want more information, know it's too soon to act, or are simply prioritizing their time and delegating tasks. These are also people who do well under pressure. They have it in them to make a decision quickly if needed.

Remember Singh from chapter 4 who was informed of the death of a child on a machine made by his company? The default in that situation would have been to swing into action and quickly call an emergency staff meeting. By going for a walk, one can say he procrastinated on his decision making. What came out of that delay was the creative idea of flying to the hospital where the incident occurred. Ultimately, that action led to unexpected wins in the form of a motivated team that took it upon themselves to improve the quality of their production processes.

Between serial procrastinators and frenzied doers, who are always ahead of schedule, lies the sweet spot of active procrastination that allows creative thought, which in turn can reveal a nonlinear path to great results.

I tend to be someone who is always ahead of schedule, especially for projects I am not experienced with. Worry makes me plan things so I will have time in case something goes wrong. In Grant's lingo, I am a "precrastinator." During the writing of this book, I gave active procrastination a shot. I chose the sale of a home to coach myself into active procrastination. My default would have been to line up the attorney, realtor, and every single thing I could think of before kicking off the sale. That kind of preparation takes time. Instead, I chose to list with a realtor first to test the market. To manage the worry that I might fall behind in finding an attorney when the time comes, I told myself that good attorneys are not hard to find for simple transactions such as mine. While I was telling myself this, I remembered that I had received a bunch of referrals from another realtor a while ago. Sure enough, the day I got a serious application from a buyer, I initiated contact with and spoke to four attorneys and made my choice in one morning.

The sale went very smoothly. Perhaps it was always going to be smooth. The difference I noticed was that I was relaxed through the process. My mind wasn't in overdrive, thinking through every eventuality and being overprepared. While there are life projects where being prepared well in advance is a good thing, it is worth challenging the habit of taking a whole bunch of premature action, out of stress and worry, in the name of being prepared.

The same idea applies to laziness. We can be lazy out of helplessness, or we can be lazy out of choice.

CLEVER AND LAZY WINS THE TOP JOB

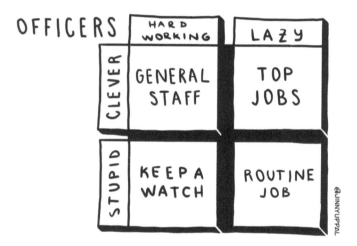

A four-class categorization of officers has been attributed to Kurt von Hammerstein-Equord, an anti-Nazi World War II German General, as a decision-making tool to select and place officers in the armed forces. He explained his logic thusly:

"I distinguish four types. There are clever, hardworking, stupid, and lazy officers. Usually, two characteristics are combined. Some are clever and hardworking; their place is the general staff. The next ones are stupid and lazy; they make up 90 percent of every army and are suited to routine duties. Anyone who is both clever and lazy is qualified for the highest leadership duties because he possesses the mental clarity and strength of nerve necessary for difficult decisions. One must beware of anyone who is both stupid and hardworking; he must not be entrusted with any responsibility because he will always only cause damage."

To understand how far this philosophy applies in a modern armed force, I turned to a senior officer in the Indian Navy who preferred to stay anonymous. He said, "In some ways the matrix is correct, even though it's a bit superficial. When you say, 'lazy,' you don't mean an ignoramus or disinterested person. You mean someone who prioritizes very well as to what is important and what is not. He is able to see the big picture and can decide, 'Okay, I am not going to sweat the small stuff.' They outsource things they are not good at. The top person in the armed forces needs to have their head uncluttered and not bogged down with detail. Their staff, on the other hand, needs to know the devil in the details."

Hammerstein-Equord was not alone in recognizing the value of the lazy person. Bill Gates reportedly has said, "I choose a lazy person to do a hard job. Because a lazy person will find an easy way to do it."

Laziness that comes from a mindset of getting results without slogging for it can very well be a winning life strategy too.

BEING LAZY LIKE A FOX

Daniel Griffiths is an unassuming Englishman. I met him while at Harvard Business School in 2009. He was among the most quiet and reserved people. He rarely participated in class. He was not to be found staying out late partying and drinking in Harvard Square along with the rest of us. When I met him, he was the managing director of a $120-million-a-year business in the United Kingdom. He was twenty-nine.

His life strategy is based on looking for shorter and more fun routes to his goals. When studying at university, he knew he wanted to be successful in business. He graduated in economics and wanted to be a director (CEO or division head equivalent) of a company. And he wanted to get there quickly. "All of the ways that people told me about how to get there," he told me, "I didn't want to do them." Those ways included putting in your time at a firm and working your way up the ranks, one promotion at a time. "I didn't want to do it because of the time it took. And because it was boring." He knew that he would likely fail at the projects middle managers were required to do. He was good at disrupting and growing a business, "not the middle-layer stuff."

So, what did he do? "I knew I had to find someone who would put me in a position of growing a business. I knew I needed to put myself next to someone like that, rather than let him see me from a distance, through his direct reports." He found such a person in the owner of a food products company. "I proved to him in a short amount of time that I could deliver on the role I wanted." Griffiths quickly landed the role he aspired to: assistant to CEO. In short order, he grew to be a Managing Director in the company and further went on to lead a successful merger and turnaround of two large family-owned businesses with a revenue of $450 million. By Griffiths's estimation, it took him three years to get to a role that normally takes twenty years after college. This was not a bleeding edge Silicon Valley technology firm; Griffiths worked in the agriculture and food products sector.

An executive coach he met years ago summed up his style this way: He is a "positioner." He positions himself and his business along fast and nonlinear paths to success. This is Griffiths's approach to everything in life and work.

In our conversation, Griffiths used self-disparaging phrases such as "cheating the system." "I look at myself as a fraud, really, you know, in not playing by the playbook. I often have an affinity with the guy in the movie *Catch Me If You Can* (where the protagonist fraudulently passes himself off as an airline pilot among other professionals).

It reminded me of other book interviews and my own experience. Some of the people who have achieved results without putting in the conventional long hours carry guilt about it. Remember van Kaam feeling guilty about taking a walk to mind-wander before a critical meeting? In one of my jobs, a common narrative among my peer executives was, "I am so busy in back-to-back meetings; I have no time to breathe." I would wonder why I was never in back-to-back meetings but was doing very well in that role and company. I'd feel like an outsider and a bit guilty in not being able to participate in the complaints of how overwhelming work life was.

Some may think Griffiths took the easy way out; he didn't put in the years to develop his leadership skills. He thinks differently. He thinks following the playbook is taking the easy way out. "It's easy to get on the treadmill. Sometimes it's just easier to get on with it [the prescribed set of actions]." It takes original thinking to find an alternate to the playbook. And, as in the case of Griffiths, the payoffs can be great: a faster path to managing director while doing the work he loves. He sums up his motto in life as this: "How do I get from A to Z? Definitely not via B to Y."

This chapter is not celebrating laziness that comes from inertia and depression. It's about ignoring the path prescribed by others in the name of work ethic or paying your dues. It's about determining where you can and want to fit in the scheme of things. It's about making your move once chance and opportunity present themselves. It's about being lazy like a fox.

IT'S ALL SOFT WORK

It can be hard to accept laziness and procrastination as positive behaviors. I think that is primarily because of our universal acknowledgment of hard work as virtuous and of laziness and procrastination as its opposing quality. It's worth examining where and how the term "hardworking" came into our lingo to begin with.

According to *Merriam-Webster*, "hardworking" was first used in 1774 at a time when the majority of the population indeed did a lot of "hard" work—physical, laborious, bone-tiring work, be it building bridges, laying down bricks, or growing crops. The industrial revolution alleviated that by introducing machines that automated the hardest and most laborious jobs. The technology revolution took automation to a whole new level. Today, most physically hard work is or can be done by machines and computers. Even farmers and growers, in the United States at least, have sophisticated machinery to take over the most labor-intensive parts of their work. Humans increasingly do soft work. Yet we use hard work in our lingo all the time; we glorify it. "Running on the hamster wheel," "getting on the treadmill," "everyday grind" are oft repeated phrases in our everyday language. *Merriam-Webster* offers this as an example of "hardworking" in a sentence: "Our students have to be very *hardworking* and committed. They put in long hours," forever tying hard work, commitment, and long hours together as if they all have to be true for any one of them to be true.

HARD WORK IN 18TH CENTURY

HARD WORK IN 21ST CENTURY

The hard work of olden times tired our bodies; the modern version of hard work tires our minds, our souls. While the scourge of that society was physical disease, the modern-day equivalent is lack of well-being in the best case and depression, anxiety, and burnout in the worst.

As urbanization and digitization across the globe grows, we are doing less and less physical work. The need in our times is soft work: creative ideas, decision making, risk taking. It is creativity that will help us stay relevant in the changing times, not mindless hard work. While there are still many professions that require physical labor, it's not a reality for most of us. It's time to stop glorifying ideas that don't add value to our lives anymore.

The deep stigma attached to laziness and procrastination is also worth challenging. It is a telling sign that when I started searching online for research on laziness, only three out of ten auto-complete suggestions had a positive association. Procrastination was worse, with only two positive associations. The negative auto-complete suggestions ranged from "is a sin," "leads to failure" (also depression/unemployment/poverty), "is the enemy of success." The one that made me smile was a very lyrical autocomplete: "Procrastination is the assassination of motivation."

Think on your own life and that of those close to you. Do you know of ethical, high integrity, successful people who are not always busy working, who seem lazy? Do you know of people who took the hard work and long hours ethic all the way into burnout, negatively impacting well-being for themselves and those that depend on them financially and emotionally?

Consider that in our times, the pendulum has swung too far toward hard work becoming a lot of doing, and that it is possible to get the very results and success we seek without all that doing. Instead of hard work, I invite you to choose work that is hard and risky. Take a chance on a new career or a break from an unfulfilling, monotonous one. Learn a brand-new skill even if you feel you are too old or too young. (Computer programming, anyone? How about writing that book you've been thinking about?) Or sign up for a project for which you have no prior experience.

Where passive procrastination and helpless laziness can feel crippling, depressing, and paralyzing, the same qualities as a choice will feel liberating. They free your mind to discover creative paths to success. It takes a certain amount of courage and confidence to put off things, especially if you are the over-prepared types, but the freedom from the stress of constant doing is rewarding in its own right. Getting off the treadmill and on the couch could be the ticket to making nonlinear jumps toward great results.

CONTEMPLATION

1. What is your opinion on the qualities of laziness and procrastination?
2. Think of two people you know well. They are both successful, ethical, and demonstrate high integrity. One is burned out; the other seems relaxed. If you can't think of people you know well, move out a degree or two of separation. How do these two people run their lives differently?

PART 4

CONCLUSION

CHAPTER 12

DECONSTRUCTING DICHOTOMIES

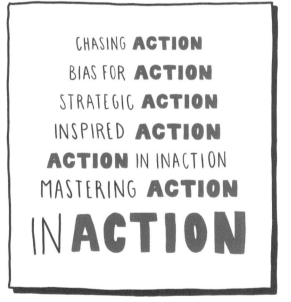

Thus far, the book has been about our action bias, the reasons why we chase action in order to pursue results, and stories of people who either fell into that trap or have found a way out of it, at least for some aspects of their lives. This book is meant to be a practical guide into understanding our action bias and what we can do about it. Hopefully you are either convinced or are starting to see the truth in what I promised to demonstrate in the Introduction:

Life is not as hard as it seems. Life is not a hamster wheel, which runs only if we keep running. Something much more than our actions makes our world go around. It is worth stopping long enough to connect with the undulating flow of life. It is worth riding the flow of life that can carry us further than we could ever go with our own "doing" alone.

This book is about mastering action, which is developing a discernment of when to act and when not to act. It's about reducing unnecessary action and leveraging inaction to drive results. While action and inaction, laziness and hard work, focused and wandering mind may seem like opposite constructs, hopefully the book has demonstrated how they can each be used to get results. This chapter is a philosophical take on further deconstructing other dichotomies that rule our thinking, including the apparent dichotomy of action and inaction.

A MULTICULTURAL DICHOTOMY IN DECISION MAKING

I grew up in India and moved to the United States in my early twenties. By that time, a lot of my worldview and conditioning had been formed. Over the next twenty plus years, I was influenced by a process of Americanization as a result of which my worldview became a mishmash of Indian and

American values. All immigrants go through this process. On the wide spectrum that is Indian-ized and American-ized, I find that each immigrant finds a unique spot depending on which cultural aspects and mindset they allowed in and which ones they kept out. You can replace Indian with Chinese, Russian, Mexican; it's an inevitable part of the immigrant integration journey. The same is true for a person who moved from Montana to Manhattan.

Having lived in or worked with people across Europe, India, and the United States, one quality I appreciate about most Americans I meet is decisiveness and conclusiveness—a quality in deep contrast with my Indian circles. For something as simple as getting a few friends/family together, the planning process in my American set is decisive. Someone takes the lead; maybe there's a quick group discussion on where to meet, choice of lunch, dinner, or drinks. And voila, a get-together happens. It is not so in my Indian context. For the first few months of writing this book, I was visiting Mumbai, my hometown. Since it was a once-in-a-lifetime event for all my siblings to be in the same physical vicinity, I planned a dinner for everyone in the apartment where I was temporarily living. After many conversations with the four sibling families (this is a consensus-driven culture; everyone has to agree with the details), the plan was finalized. The formal reason was to kick off my niece's wedding coming up in a few weeks.

The day after the plan was settled, one of my sisters texted me, "Some plans changed; call me when you are awake." We were going to her home instead. Saturday dinner had now become a Sunday brunch. She told me about a ritual among her in-laws wherein the bride-to-be along with the family was invited for a meal. She wanted to combine my gathering with that. She had already informed the others. My first reaction was: where did that come from? Why was this "ritual" not brought up before? Why am I, the host, being informed and not consulted? After huffing and puffing for a while, I realized that what really bothered me was the change, not the new plan. In reality, decades after moving away, I was happy to just be in India, close to family, for months at a time. What did it really matter where we met? Alright, let's go with the flow.

A day before the brunch, said sister felt too ill to cook. Refusing to give up easily, she had to be convinced to either move the venue to a restaurant or allow us to bring food. Another flurry of phone calls and texts later, we decided, the evening before the scheduled brunch, to meet in a restaurant. At the restaurant we ran into an entire branch of cousins who just happened to be eating there. Our gathering doubled in size and became a major party. They had all not seen each other for over a year due to the COVID-19 pandemic, and I had not seen these cousins since my last visit more than two years prior.

The utter fluidity of the planning process was disconcerting to me. And yet, no one could have planned for the gathering that it turned out to be. After months of being cooped up in apartment buildings with no outdoor space due to the pandemic, I felt like a wide-eyed child in the expanse of the huge restaurant. Seeing many of my cousins unexpectedly was a huge bonus.

The weeks and months I spent in India while writing this book made the difference between the decisiveness and indecisiveness of my two worlds very vivid. The decision-making process in my Indian context evolves in small increments, meandering its way to usually a great outcome—albeit, in my eyes, highly inefficiently. Had I stayed hung up with the goal of gathering everyone at my place, the actual outcome (brunch at restaurant) would have felt disappointing. Once I evolved my goal to just *be* with family, then this outcome far exceeded the goal, and the definition of family got expanded to include cousins.

Indians often use a phrase to make fun of themselves: "Ram Bharose Hindu Hotel." It signifies a hotel of that name, which is run by their owners entirely on faith (*bharose* in Hindi) in Lord Ram, a Hindu God. This philosophy has no marketing, no business plan, no roadmap, just faith. That's one end of the spectrum.

I lean closer to the other end, like many Americans in business. I like predictability and order. I like confidence and clarity when thinking and communicating about the future. At least give me that in an upcoming dinner! My own action bias stems from the need to create that predictable world order. The pandemic and the time spent in India was a challenging but timely experience to let go of the desire of predictability and order and trust that life will lead me to great results, even when it looks like it's going off track.

DICHOTOMY IN EXPERTS' OPINIONS

While conducting research for this book, I ran into another dichotomy to do with research itself.

Social psychology books have become wildly popular in the last fifteen years or so. Books such as *Blink, Grit, Think Again*, and many others have had the effect of opening my mind to newer facts about why we think the way we think and why we do what we do. Unfortunately, for every research-based finding or "facts" from an expert, counterpoints eventually emerge from other experts.

I loved Malcom Gladwell's *Blink* when I read it in the late 2000s. Gladwell writes, "The first task of *Blink* is to convince you of a simple fact: decisions made very quickly can be every bit as good as decisions made cautiously and deliberately." A few years later, I attended a negotiations course with Harvard Business School professor Max Bazerman. He emphatically declared that Gladwell's recommendations in his book were misleading and harmful, especially in negotiations. In his mind, Gladwell "ignored the detrimental impact of many other significant cognitive biases: overconfidence, the tendency to escalate commitment to a chosen course of action, the undue influence of vivid information." In other words, our intuition is flawed due to our biases and blind spots. Relying on that intuition to take action is perpetuating flawed thinking.

Similarly, noted author Angela Duckworth wrote a treatise on grit, passion, and perseverance in her book. Can you guess its name? *Grit*. On the other hand, organizational psychologist Adam Grant, in his book *Think Again*, points to the dark side of grit: "There's a fine line between heroic persistence and foolish stubbornness." Gritty mountaineers, he says, are more likely to die on expeditions due to their determination to reach the summit.

Who is a layperson to believe? And what am I supposed to do with all these contradictions as I write my book?

I reached out to Adam Grant, who has authored multiple books on behavioral science with my question: "How do you personally rationalize between all these ideologies? It seems no matter what I want to say, I can find data or do my own research to prove it. It's a little bit of a conundrum since I am citing other people's research in my book and not doing my own extensive research."

He replied, "I'd say none of these theories are wrong—the goal is to find the conditions when they're right." He also sent me a *New York Times* opinion piece, aptly called, "Possible Limits on Science of Behavior." I sent him back this response with a quote from the paper: "This does it for me: 'Anyone who views social psychology research as a means of uncovering generalizations fails to perceive its most important function: the delineation of limits or boundaries.'"

Apart from completely flipping the intrinsic value of research, what this means is that nothing is generally or always true. Even if it is true for many, it may not be true for you or your specific situation. Going back to the chapter on Default Action Playbook, relying on established playbooks limits possibilities. It may seem there is one best way, because of the book you just read or what the influencer you follow says over and over or the specific news feed you read. But it isn't so.

Experts and other successful people are not always right, and their findings are not always black and white. Moreover, as we will see in the next chapter, you yourself know more than you think you do.

(COLLAPSING THE) DICHOTOMY OF ACTION AND INACTION

How does any of this apply to action and inaction? Despite what the title or marketing for this book may suggest, it isn't a conclusive or decisive guide on when to take action or not. As is the case in the sections above, an invitation here is to acknowledge that just as people are far more layered than we think, life is far more textured than we realize. The stories in this book notwithstanding, there is no ultimate ten-step conclusive formula to identify what is the right action and what is not. There is, however, a way of being that puts us in touch with our own inner guidance system. I will turn to *Bhagavad Gita*, an ancient Indian text, for help explaining it.

Bhagavad Gita is a comprehensive guide on the theory of karma, on action and inaction. It has inspired many modern thinkers and luminaries such as Mahatma Gandhi, Henry David Thoreau, Carl Jung, and George Harrison, among others. According to many scholars, verse 18 from chapter 4 of the *Gita* captures the essence of the entire text. It certainly captures what this book is saying.

कर्मण्यकर्म यः परयेदकर्मणि च कर्म यः
स बुद्धिमान्मनुष्येषु स युक्तः कृत्स्नकर्मकृत्

karmaṇyakarma yaḥ paśhyed akarmaṇi
ćha karma yaḥ sa buddhimān manuṣhyeṣhu
sa yuktaḥ kṛitsna-karma-kṛit

Those who see action in inaction and
inaction in action are truly wise amongst humans.
Although performing all kinds of actions, they are
yogis and masters of all their actions.

@JINNYUPPAL

Bhagavad Gita, Chapter 4, Verse 18

Let's dig into this verse one sentence at a time.

*Those who see action in inaction and inaction in action
are truly wise amongst humans.*

Although it sounds like a clever tongue twister, this phrase
is deeply profound. It took me many years to fully grasp the
meaning and application of this in life. I invite you to read
this section slowly, taking as many pauses as you like.

The first part of the first sentence, *action in inaction*, is
easier to unpack. As the neuroscientist Raichle said when
talking about the Default Mode Network in the chapter on
daydreaming and mind-wandering, our brain is active even
when we are doing nothing. Similarly, our internal organs

keep doing their thing, while we are in inaction, for example when we are sleeping. Inaction is never all there is; action is happening somewhere in there.

Going back to the introduction of this book, in the middle of the seemingly unproductive, lazy periods of my life, action was occurring. It wasn't visible to me, but the seeds of action were being sown, to be manifested in due course. As a recent example, the idea of this book was born during my outwardly underproductive phase during a pandemic when I didn't have a full-time job and was homebound. Amid inaction, there is always action.

The reverse, *inaction in action*, took longer before I truly understood it. This can be interpreted in a few ways.

It is the silence in between the notes that make the song. It is the space between these very words that makes the sentence readable.

A more practical interpretation is setting an intention and vision versus goal setting. It's the mission and values of a business and not its annual targets.

It's what people say about you in your obituary versus what's on your resume. It's who you *are*, not what you *do*.

But that is not what this phrase is about. At least that's not all it is about.

Seeing inaction in action is an acknowledgement of non-doership. Let me elaborate. In fall 2008, I attended a talk series at Art of Living, the organization where I first learned my meditation practice. In this format, the facilitator would play a recording of a talk or discourse, and we would discuss it as a group afterwards. One particular session in this series was titled, *"You are not the doer."*

Recall from chapter 3 that my entry into meditation and spiritual practices was fraught with skepticism. This was during that phase. By the end of the recording and brief remarks from the facilitator, I was ready for debate. "What do you mean I am not the doer? Let me give you a simple example," I said. "What if the doorbell rings, and no one is at home other than me. If I don't get up and open the door, a 'doing', the person on the other side can't get in. I have to 'do,' take action, for things to move along. How am I not the doer here?" Others joined in with their doubts, and a hearty discussion followed. What about taking action to prevent a wrong from happening. Isn't taking action the same thing as taking responsibility? Aren't we the doer in that case? What about leadership? Being a good leader means being unafraid to take action, doing what it takes. The discussion didn't seem to land anywhere specific. I left that session unconvinced.

Some years and many meditations later as I was thinking of that session, a simple change in emphasis in the statement "You are not the doer" jumped out.

What if I write it as such:

You are not **THE** doer.

Did anything pop for you?

Consider the idea that action is happening *through* you, not *from* you. Going back to the doorbell, a whole host of circumstances were created to put me on this side of the door and the other person on the outside. All sorts of events occurred for me to have the opportunity to open the door. I had limbs, arms, and legs enough to walk over and open it. I was trained to hear the sound of the bell and knew what it meant.

I was not *the* doer. I was *a participant.*

So it is that in this game of life, my job is not to do as much as it is to participate. Recognizing that allows me to see inaction in my own action. I am not *the one* taking action; action is happening *through* me.

Take that in for a moment.

An immediate reaction to the "You are not the doer" philosophy may be, "Okay, so does that mean I should give up taking action? Should I stop trying and leave it to the gods?" We, humans, have no choice but to act; we are wired to act. Action bias is not a bad thing. It's our nature. It's the nature of all existence. No bias needs to be overcome.

Pause and take *that* in.

Now for the last phrase in this verse.

Although performing all kinds of actions, they are yogis and masters of all their actions.

A yogi is one who acts without taking on doership. Elsewhere, the *Gita* elaborates that a yogi does not feel attached or entitled to the action nor the fruit of the action (outcome). The yogi is not enslaved to her actions nor the outcome. She is not chasing action; she is not chasing outcomes.

The yogi is a master of her actions.

This verse from the *Gita* kicks this conversation up several notches. This book has been saying that mastering action is about rising above both action and inaction; it is about knowing when to act and when not to act. It positions inaction as a mechanism to get to the place where you will automatically know when to act and when not to act.

The *Gita* builds up to a more evolved guidance: a complete detachment from the outcome puts you in a state of mind where you see that action and inaction are intertwined deeply. You realize that no choice is to be made between acting or not; you show up for life and flow with it. You don't do. You just are. It's a beautiful place to be, I imagine. I don't live there. In my deepest moments of silence and meditation, I have had a glimpse of it. That's how I know how powerful and beautiful that place is. But that's not where I live all the time. So, I needed to create a mindset within the life I do live to take me a step closer and to keep me there. Moments of inaction and pause, in the middle of all the doing, take me and other protagonists in this book closer to the place of creativity where things just seem to click in place on their own. This book, then, becomes a step in the direction of the life the *Gita* is asking us to live.

So now what? All this may still sound a bit esoteric. Let's say we have some things to accomplish in the near future. Life is coming at us fast. How on earth does all this apply to daily life?

Let's end this book on a bit more, *ahem*, actionable note.

CHAPTER 13

THE PRACTICE OF MASTERING ACTION

———

Masters of any creative or performing art, be it sculpting, classical music, or dance, will often tell you that after years or decades of performing, they are "just now beginning to get the hang of it." It's the fans and the media who call the performer a master. The master, on the other hand, is aware that she or he is but a practitioner, a lifelong student.

So, it is with mastering action. It is not a "one and done" event; it's not something you acquire once and are set for life. Rather, it's a lifelong practice.

Unlike the creative arts, it doesn't take years or decades to build a mastery of action. It takes but a New York minute to recognize our action bias. A simple pause and inquiry, "Am I doing this for the sake of doing?" "Is this action really needed here?" yanks us out of barreling down the doing path.

This mastery is accessible to us all, at all times, regardless of age, background, and any other limitations we think we have. No one else has arrived any more than you. Those who seem to have mastered action did so in that situation, in that aspect of their lives. So, it is in your life. In some parts of your life, you seem to have the right judgment on when to act and when not to. In other parts, it's a bit of a mess.

This book is meant to be descriptive and not prescriptive. I wrote it to open our minds to an alternative, nonlinear path to results, different from the traditional path of hard work equating to long hours, mental fatigue, and burnout. As much as I wrote this book for you, dear friend, I also wrote it for myself. While outwardly I appear calm and self-assured (I say this based on feedback I am often given), it takes work for me to overcome my most natural tendency to want to control life and situations through my actions and the worry, which follows when things don't go my way.

I have tried many of the approaches in this book with varying degrees of success while writing and publishing this book, a major project in anyone's life. I have shared my experiences over time in this book, on my social channels, as well as in book newsletters.

If you have read this far and are still not convinced with the book's thesis, then I invite you to try an experiment to see for yourself if any of the ideas in this book do something for you. If it works, good for you. If it doesn't, then drop the subject for now. No one is a better expert on your life than you.

If you have come this far and are a believer, then I invite you to pick an area of life where you are not applying this approach. No matter your beliefs, action bias is a most innate human tendency. You will discover an area in your life that could use a different approach.

Before we get to the takeaways from the book, let's prime our minds first.

YOU KNOW MORE THAN YOU THINK YOU DO

Consider the world of things we know and don't know. Usually, we are quite clear on things we know that we know. I know how to build teams and drive business growth or how to write a book. It's also easy to list out the things that we don't know. I am aware that I don't know how to code in Python, how to make Indian mango pickle, and about a gazillion other specific things. To move things from the second circle to the first circle, I can take classes or self-train to acquire that knowledge.

Next, we have things we don't know that we don't know. This is where our ignorance and blind spots live. In one of my fast-paced technology roles; it was common for leaders, including me, to present our plans, projections, risks, pros, and cons, ending with a philosophical, "Beyond this, we don't know what we don't know." Stating that truth was a way of acknowledging that things could go really well or wrong but that I have no way of accounting for it right now. This is also where our subconscious biases and blind prejudice live. We can import things from this circle into what we know by either living through life and/or taking personal development courses that give us deep insight into our biases and psyche.

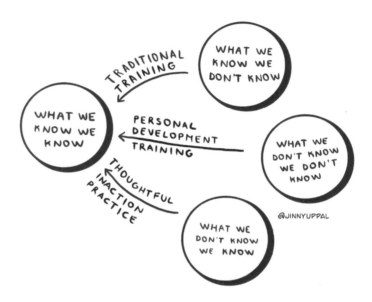

We now come to the most magical circle. This is the world of things we know but are not in our conscious awareness. A deeper part of us is far more connected with the universe, and all its inhabitants and ideas and solutions, than we know. This is where intuition and deep creativity lives. Possibilities dwell here. This book is about building your springboard to operate in that space. Taking a break from nonstop action can be that springboard.

With that possibility in mind, let's now take steps to enter that space.

Ready?

STEP 1: ACKNOWLEDGE

Acknowledge that you, like all humans, are susceptible to action bias.

Acknowledge that you do know how to manage it. You've done it before, somewhere, sometime in your life.

Acknowledge that while our bias for action is a basic behavioral tendency, it manifests by showing up in micro-moments. That's where the action is, no pun intended. This will reduce the size of the issue we are dealing with, making it less threatening. No major psychological surgery is needed here.

STEP 2: ACCEPT

Accept that nothing is wrong here or with you. If your action or inaction seemingly led to undesirable outcomes in the past, that's okay. It will probably happen again. And that's all right too.

Accept that you are not alone in this. No matter how put-together someone else seems in their social media life, he or she is in the same boat as you.

Accept that mastering action is not about having or creating a perfect life. It's about discovering and observing how easily we slip into unnecessary action. It's about being aware of those moments without judgment, sometimes in advance, thereby intercepting the action, or after the fact and learning a lesson from them.

STEP 3: PICK AN AREA OF LIFE TO WORK ON

Pick a time-bound, upcoming project where you think your action bias tendency might get in the way and you'd like to practice using a different approach. You would like to develop the muscle to know what it feels like to leverage inaction. If you see results, you will automatically want to try it again and for bigger things in life.

You could choose a job search, fundraising for your startup or nonprofit, an upcoming pitch, transitioning into a new life, city, role, or work environment. Your life is rich with opportunities!

Choose something that will be hard enough but not something where your life or career hangs in balance. In the latter case, the risk is that you might become action obsessed in applying this book's learnings!

Choose something in your life without relying on someone else to partner up with you. If success depends on someone else trying this book's ideas along with you, then you are at risk of being distracted by their choices.

Trust that you will come up with your own uniquely designed springboard to the place of creative ideas. What this book can do for you is serve as a kick-starter. As you read the summary takeaways below, think of two or three that appeal to you the most. Don't overthink it. Some of these will jump out right away. Those are the approaches to try on. If it feels right, go back and re-read the chapter listed after the takeaway for more inspiration.

SUMMARY TAKEAWAYS

GOAL SETTING

1. The Principles Filter: Write down your goals as clearly as you can. Then run them by your principles filter. If you have written principles, great. If not, that's fine. Principles don't become principles only when you can write them down in crisp, pithy slogans. You know what yours are. Will any of the goals compromise your principles? For example, time with family or your cherished nonprofit work or hobby? Is it missing elements which make you happy and fulfilled? If so, revisit the goal.

2. Broaden your goals: Inevitably, your first set of goals are going to be narrow. What dimensions are you missing? You can draw from your principles. If the goal is to "build a great team," can you add "gender, racial, skills, and professional background diversity" to it? Run it by someone who can challenge your thinking.

3. Revisit goals often. Life is a long game. For most of us, it is hard to imagine and envision our entire lives and opportunities ahead of us. Thankfully, life is too dynamic for five- or ten-year goals. The same is the case for your short-term project. Revisit goals often. Just as it is worthwhile to broaden our goals, it is also useful to let go of some short-term wins, while we stay focused on longer-term ones.

Chapters to re-read: Principles vs. Goals and Breaking Through the Paradox of Goal Setting.

4. Define the outcome you want and alter the playbook: You probably had a playbook in mind to get to the outcome. It either came from something you tried in the past, something an expert or a guru has been preaching, or something you feel bound by (for example, the norm in your industry). Tyler Hayes is a three-time startup Silicon Valley founder who turned to crowdfunding to raise funds for his fourth business. He did it at a time when venture and angel fundraising was (and is) the norm for startups. When the crowdfunding campaign was over, his team significantly exceeded their goals and also saved themselves the frustration and emotional exhaustion that comes from innumerable pitches and inevitable rejections in the traditional fundraising path. What might you try differently?

Chapters to re-read: The Default Action Playbook and Principles-Based Action Playbook.

MAKE ROOM FOR CHANCE

5. As chance events occur and new insights or information become available, be open to revisiting your goals and action plans.

Chapter to re-read: The Chance Effect.

TRY A NEW CREATIVE SPRINGBOARD

6. Allow yourself time during your day or week to let your mind wander. Once you've made the time and decided

you won't feel guilty about it, no other intervention or preparation is required. No need to take notes the moment an interesting thought comes up. If your mind starts worrying or starts obsessing, then stop. Otherwise, let your mind roam free. Afterward, harvest for interesting thoughts you want to explore further.

7. Procrastinate. Get bold: give active procrastination a try! Pick a decision or task which is important and requires work from your side. If your normal default is to jump into doing or start worrying about it, postpone your self-imposed deadline. Renegotiate deadlines with others if you need to. Walk away from it entirely until it's time to pick it back up. See what new information came up that you can incorporate into your action.

8. Choose to be lazy. Pick a job or task you want done. If you wanted to minimize the work it will take from your side, what would you do? Outsource? Automate? What's the worst that will happen if you skip it?

9. Practice silence. Pick one upcoming conversation: an interview, a meeting, or a negotiation. Declare upfront that you may pause every now and then before responding. You can share with your audience that if you do pause, it is to be sure you understand the other person and want to be thoughtful in your responses. This will set expectations so others don't rush in to fill the silence and will create trust in your intent. Then authentically pause when it feels right. This is not the place to fake it until you make it. If silence doesn't feel natural, pick another time, another place.

10. If meditation has been on your mind, give it a try. Commit to meditating for twenty minutes every day for forty consecutive days. Avoid too many props such as incense,

sound bath, spiritual altars, etc. Trust that your mind and your breath are all the tools you need for now. If your mind wanders during meditation, that's fine. Bring it back to the breath when you notice it has wandered. Don't over analyze your meditations or post about them on social media; let this be your private practice for now.

Chapters to re-read: The Rise (and Irony) of the Self-Awareness Era, Power of Silence, Daydreaming and Mind-wandering As Creative Tools, Being Lazy and Procrastinating Your Way to Results.

OTHER THOUGHTS: ANCHORING IN YOURSELF

11. Pick a habit that is restorative and encourages self-reflection in you. Walking, journaling, meditation, painting, reading. Whatever already works for you is the best for you. If you are inspired to do so, add something that has worked in the past but is not in your lifestyle at the moment.

12. Learn to read your physical and mental signals. The more ambition you have on a topic, the more likely you are to develop urgency. Sometimes the urgency will be timely, and sometimes it will misguide. Learn your own signals when the ambition and urgency are taking you across the line into thoughtless doing. It could be a physical sensation or the voice in your head. Look back to Herre van Kaam's description in the chapter on mind-wandering of how he feels in a meeting when things are going well versus when they are not. My own physical signals are a tightening in the body and face, sometimes accompanied

by a feeling of a rush in the body. What are yours? Take a break if you are getting a negative signal.

13. To get past an obsessive attachment to an outcome, consider the worst-case scenario. What if it doesn't go your way? What might happen? And then what might happen? Run it to the end state. I find that writing worst-case scenarios slows down thoughts, giving me time to critically examine them. Most likely, you've either been in the worst-case scenario before or have gotten close. Write about that time and situation. Didn't you live to tell the tale? I once used the phrase "all outcomes are acceptable" like a mantra when planning my action path in a matter with high stakes. I achieved the outcome I had so urgently wanted, but more importantly it tempered my own tension and gave me confidence in the actions I took. Moreover, it helped me develop a plan B if it went badly. And it made the journey to the actual outcome more enjoyable.

I am curious if any of this helped you. If anything in this book has inspired you or triggered a change in your thinking, tell me about it! You can write on my social channels *@jinnyuppal* or on my website *jinnyuppal.com*. This is one action I hope you do take!

ACKNOWLEDGMENTS

To start with, I acknowledge you for taking a big step toward embracing the power of thoughtful inaction.

They say it takes a village to make a book. Well, I have no idea if anybody actually said that, but it is so! The village who helped shape this book is very large, and I may not do justice in naming everybody. Nonetheless, a few stand out whom I'd like to acknowledge.

Ricardo Khan put the idea of writing a book into my head and gently persisted until I took it seriously. The result is here for you to see.

Payal and her husband Pradeep Surve generously gave me full use of their vacant furnished apartment in Mumbai for several months during my visit. That beautiful and serene apartment was the scene of my decision to write the book and where part of the manuscript was written.

My coaches and publishing team at Creator's Institute and New Degree Press: Eric Koester, Scott Aronowitz, John

Saunders, Brian Bies, and Carol McKibben, among many others, were incredible in teaching me the ins and outs of storytelling, book writing, and publishing. They showed up for me every step of the way in a flawless choreography of this journey, which lasted less than twelve months from the decision to write the book to the publish date.

I'd like to acknowledge my earliest alpha readers and supporters Ajit Singh and Navjeet Bawa for their support and their feedback. Divya Kaur not only supported me throughout the journey but talked me off the ledge many times, especially when I just didn't want the bother of marketing and promoting the book.

My author community is a diverse group of people from sixteen countries who preordered the book; their faith gave me wings and motivated me to produce the best work I possibly could. Their names are further below. Among them, I'd like to call out my beta readers who gave me beautifully detailed feedback on chapters: Alison Pyle, Greg Dowty, Julie Elmore, Julz Amidala, Jyoti Malik, Manohar Bhambhani, Padma Satish, Rani Nagpal, Sarah Bierenbaum.

Eva Hilf, Dan Driscoll, Jasmine Narula, Pavita Singh, and Shilpa Bhandari moderated lively and fun book talks with my early supporters and author community. Eva Hilf gave me the idea of the book title. Guntaas Kaur Uppal helped keep citations complete and accurate, giving me one less thing to be bothered about.

I am grateful to this amazing group of people who made up my author community, supporting me and my work well before it was published.

Aakanksha Surve

Adam Wiener

Ajit Singh

Akash Chhabra

Alison Pyle

Allison Hale

Aman Sood

Amory Houghton

Anchita Monga

Andrew Latham

Aniket Gune

Anu Nistala

Anu Sethi

Aparna Iyer

Archana Turaga

Ashish Nangla

Avinash Mehrotra

Beth Grossfeld

Betsy Martin

Bhuvaneshwari Krishnamoorthy

Brendan Stewart

Carlo Mahfouz

Carrie Collins

Carrie Weaver

Chandrasekhar Movva

Dan Driscoll

Dana Gilland

Daniel Griffiths

David Guo

David Page

Dipika Verma

Divya Kaur

Donna Quinn

Elizabeth Krajewski

Emmylou Aben

Eric Koester

Eva Boyd

Farley Nachemin

Francis Adjodha

Giuliana Isaksen

Guntaas-Kaur Uppal

Gwen Kollar

Hajime Aota

Jacquie Stovern

Jagjit Toor

Jaime Ellis

James Deaton

James Vallejos

Jasmine Narula

Jason Bennewith

JD Singh

Jessica Begen

Jignasha Thakkar

Joe Lalonde

Joyce Patrick

JP Bewley
Juju Thukral
Julie Elmore
Juliet Coye
Jyoti Malik
Jyoti Singh
Kanwaldeep Bedi
Karan Yaramada
Kate McNally
Katrina Calinisan
Keiko Shigehisa
Kushal Choksi
Lisa Mendez
Lorraine Figueroa
Lovely Singh
Mahesh Kothurkar
Mahesh Subramanian
Mahesh M. Thakur
Mamta Narain
Manohar Bhambhani
Marci Weisler
Mark FelcanSmith
Mark Fraser
Matthew Willox
Megha Moza
Melanie Pitson
Michael Lin
Michelle Ferguson
Michelle Jones
Mo Rajani
Mohammad Khan
Monisha Somji

Nancy Helman
Navjeet Bawa
Navjit Bhasin
Padma Satish
Palak Mulji
Pankaj Mandpe
Parneet Gosal
Paru Radia
Patrick Pitre
Pavita Singh
Payal Surve
Praveen Chandra
Rahul Deshmukh
Rahul Sharma
Raj Yarlagadda
Ramesh Iyer
Rani Nagpal
Renee Dineen
Reshmi Nair
Richard Kane
Roger G Dowty
Ross Richman
Roz McNulty
Sai Venkateshwaran
Salem Almutawa
Sanjeev Uppal
Sanjeev Singh
Sarah Bierenbaum
Seema Chopra
Sharon Joseph
Shavonne Dargan
Shelley Poe

Shilpa Bhandari
Shubhra Bhatnagar
Siddharth Swaroop
Snigdha Nandipati
Srikanth Sunkari
Subu Desaraju
Sujatha Bhaskara
Summer Koide
Sunny Thakkar
Surbhi Chhabra
Suresh Kumar

Susan Gibson
Sven Tarantik
Timothy Perna
Trisha Surve
Usha-Kiran Chabra
Vanessa Liu
Ven Swaminathan
Vikas Mukhi
Vikram Tandon
Wendy Ellington
Yogesh Danak

BIBLIOGRAPHY

_____

INTRODUCTION

Essig, Todd. "When 'Study Drugs' Kill (Part 1): How Ambition Becomes Adderall Addiction." *Forbes,* February 10, 2013. *https://www.forbes.com/sites/toddessig/2013/02/10/when-study-drugs-kill-part-1-how-ambition-becomes-adderall-addiction/?sh=39eb21973cd1.*

Greenspan, Jesse. "Why Napoleon's Invasion of Russia Was the Beginning of the End." History, June 22, 2012. *https://www.history.com/news/napoleons-disastrous-invasion-of-russia.*

Lisa, Andrew. "30 College Majors That Didn't Exist 50 Years Ago." Stacker. Accessed on June 8, 2021. *https://stacker.com/stories/3497/30-college-majors-didnt-exist-50-years-ago.*

Pega, Frank et al. "Global, Regional, and National Burdens of Ischemic Heart Disease and Stroke Attributable to Exposure to Long Working Hours for 194 Countries, 2000–2016: A Systematic Analysis from the WHO/ILO Joint Estimates of the Work-Related Burden of Disease and Injury." Environment International, September 2021. *https://www.sciencedirect.com/science/article/pii/S0160412021002208.*

Public Affairs, UC Berkeley. "Wealth, Power or Lack Thereof at Heart of Many Mental Disorders." Accessed on September 12, 2021. *https://news.berkeley.edu/2014/12/09/dominancebehavior/.*

Tzu, Sun. *The Art of War.* Translated by Lionel Giles. London: Arcturus Publishing Ltd, 2010.

CHAPTER 1: AMBITION AND THE ACTION BIAS

Encyclopedia.com. s.v. "Action Figure." Accessed September 15, 2021, *https://www.encyclopedia.com/manufacturing/news-wires-white-papers-and-books/action-figure.*

Martin, Philip, dir. *The Crown.* Season 2, Episode 1, "Misadventure." Aired November 8, 2017, on Netflix. *https://www.netflix.com/title/80025678.*

Patt, A. and R. Zeckhauser. "Action Bias and Environmental Decisions." *Journal of Risk and Uncertainty* 21, (2000): 45–72. *https://doi.org/10.1023/A:1026517309871.*

CHAPTER 2: THE LIGHT AT THE END OF THE ACTION BIAS TUNNEL

Beard, George Miller. *American Nervousness: Its Causes and Consequences, a Supplement to Nervous Exhaustion (Neurasthenia).* New York City: Creative Media Partners, LLC, 2019.

Covey, Stephen R. *The 7 Habits of Highly Effective People: Restoring the Character Ethic.* New York City: Free Press, 2004.

Laub, Zachary. "Hate Speech on Social Media: Global Comparisons." *Council for Foreign Relations.* Last updated June 7, 2019. *https://www.cfr.org/backgrounder/hate-speech-social-media-global-comparisons.*

Soltes, Eugene F. *Why They Do It: Inside the Mind of the White-Collar Criminal.* New York City: Public Affairs, 2016.

CHAPTER 3: THE RISE (AND IRONY) OF THE SELF-AWARENESS ERA

Advisory Board. "The Mindfulness App Headspace Is Booming. But Is It Actually Effective?" Accessed on September 12, 2021. *https://www.advisory.com/en/daily-briefing/2020/08/14/mindfulness-app.*

Dineen, Renee. "Authentic Inaction: Undoing the Doing in a Do-Crazy World." Filmed February 2020 in North Adams, Ted Video, 16.18. *https://www.ted.com/talks/renee_dineen_authentic_inaction_undoing_the_doing_in_a_do_crazy_world.*

Encyclopedia Britannica Online. s.v. "Bhagwan Shree Rajneesh." Accessed on September 19, 2021, *https://www.britannica.com/biography/Bhagwan-Shree-Rajneesh.*

Goodreads. "Ernest Hemingway, Quotes, Quotable Quote." Accessed on October 1, 2021. *https://www.goodreads.com/quotes/12845-never-confuse-movement-with-action.*

Globalnewswire. "Meditation Market 2020 Edition Report with Impact of COVID-19|Top Leaders-Smiling Mind Headspace INC, Inner Explorer, Committee for Children., Stop, Breathe & Think." Accessed on May 28, 2021. *https://www.globenewswire.com/news-release/2020/06/22/2051509/0/en/Meditation-Market-2020-Edition-Report-with-Impact-of-COVID-19-Top-Leaders-Smiling-Mind-HEADSPACE-INC-Inner-Explorer-Committee-for-Children-Stop-Breathe-Think.html.*

Headspace. "Research Shows Headspace Works." Accessed on September 12, 2021. https://www.headspace.com/science/meditation-research.

Lahtinen, Oskari, Jenni Aaltonen, Johanna Kaakinen, Lena Franklin, and Jukka Hyönä. "The Effects of App-Based Mindfulness

Practice on the Well-Being of University Students and Staff." *Current Psychology*, 1-10. (May 1, 2021). Doi:10.1007/s12144-021-01762-Z.

Lassi With Lavina. "Spirituality 101—The Journey of a Skeptic." Accessed on September 22, 2021. *https://www.lassiwithlavina. com/features/faith/spirituality-101-the-journey-of-a-skeptic/ html*.

Merriam Webster Online. s.v. "Definition for Writer's Block." Accessed on September 12, 2021. *https://www.merriam-webster. com/dictionary/writer%27s%20block*.

Osin, Evgeny N. and Irina I. Turilina. "Mindfulness Meditation Experiences of Novice Practitioners in an Online Intervention: Trajectories, Predictors, and Challenges." *International Association of Applied Psychology* (15 July 2021). *https://doi.org/10.1111/ aphw.12293*.

Petersen, Andrea. "The Virtuous Midlife Crisis." *Wall Street Journal*, January 12, 2020. *https://www.wsj.com/articles/the-virtuous-midlife-crisis-11578830400*.

Swain, Thomas A, and Gerald Mcgwin. "Yoga-Related Injuries in the United States from 2001 to 2014." *Orthopaedic Journal of Sports Medicine* Vol. 4,11 2325967116671703 (16 Nov. 2016). 10.1177/2325967116671703.

"Why There's So Much Money in Mindfulness." *Quartz*, January 19, 2021. *https://qz.com/1958593/covid-19-accelerated-the-worlds-embrace-of-meditation-apps/*.

CHAPTER 4: THE DEFAULT ACTION PLAYBOOK

Bar-Eli, Michael, Ofer Azar, Ilana Ritov, Yael Keidar-Levin, and Galit Schein. "Action Bias among Elite Soccer Goalkeepers:

The Case of Penalty Kicks." *Journal of Economic Psychology*, 28 (2007): 606-621. 10.1016/J.joep.2006.12.001.

Bresiger, Gregory. "This Is How Much Time Employees Spend Slacking Off." *New York Post*, July 29, 2017. *https://nypost. com/2017/07/29/this-is-how-much-time-employees-spend-slack-ing-off/*.

Goldsmith, James. *If You See a Bandwagon, It's Too Late*. Published Independently, 2020.

Kiderman A, Ilan U, Gur I, Bdolah-Abram T, and Brezis M. "Unexplained Complaints in Primary Care: Evidence of Action Bias." *Journal of Family Practice*, Vol. 62, No. 8 (2013): 408-13. *https:// pubmed.ncbi.nlm.nih.gov/24143333/*.

Lunden, Ingrid. "Cyber Monday Came in at $10.8b Spent Online in the US, at the Low End of the Range but Still a Record One-Day Total." *Techcrunch*, November 30, 2020. *https://techcrunch. com/2020/11/30/cyber-monday-2020/*.

Pilvi Tikala. "The Trainee, 2008." Accessed May 23, 2021. *https:// pilvitakala.com/the-trainee*.

CHAPTER 5: A PRINCIPLES-BASED ACTION PLAYBOOK

Dalio, Ray. *Principles: Life and Work*. New York City: Simon & Schuster, 2017.

Grant, Adam. "The Surprising Habits of Original Thinkers." Filmed February 2016 in Vancouver, Ted Video, 15:15. *https:// www.ted.com/talks/adam_grant_the_surprising_habits_of_ original_thinkers?language=en#t-8023*.

CHAPTER 6: PRINCIPLES VS. GOALS

Breakthrough Quotes. "Quotes by Sam Walton." Accessed on September 21, 2021. *https://breakthroughquotes.com/quote_authors/sam-walton/.*

Buffet, Warren. Warren Buffet to Limited Partners, 1957. In the General Stock Market Picture in 1957. *https://www.safalniveshak.com/wp-content/uploads/2013/12/Warren-Buffett-Berkshire-Letters-1957-2012.pdf.*

Davis, L.J. "Buffet Takes Stock." *The New York Times,* April 1, 1990. *https://www.nytimes.com/1990/04/01/magazine/buffet-takes-stock.html?pagewanted=all.*

MorningConsult. *How America's Largest, Most Diverse, Best-Educated, and Most Financially Powerful Generation Will Shape the Future.* Accessed on May 27, 2021. *https://morningconsult.com/form/gen-z-report-download/.*

StockInvesting.today. *The 1969 Bear Market.* Accessed May 23, 2021. *https://stockinvesting.today/ma1607/article/the-1969-bear-market?.*

CHAPTER 7: BREAKING THROUGH THE PARADOX OF GOAL SETTING

Christensen, Clayton M. "How Will You Measure Your Life?" *Harvard Business Review,* July–August 2010. *https://hbr.org/2010/07/how-will-you-measure-your-life.*

Collins, Jim and Jerry I. Porras. *Built to Last: Successful Habits of Visionary Companies.* New York: HarperBusiness, 3rd Edition, 2011.

Kay, John. *Obliquity: Why Our Goals Are Best Achieved Indirectly.* New York: Gildan Media Corp, 2010.

Kilgore, Bruce M. "Origin and History of Wildland Fire Use in the U.S. National Park System." *The George Wright Forum.* Accessed on May 28, 2021. *http://www.georgewright.org/243kilgore.pdf.*

McIntyre, Georgia. "What Percentage of Small Businesses Fail? (And Other Need-to-Know Stats)." *Fundera* (blog). Updated on November 20, 2020. Accessed on October 1, 2021. *https://www.fundera.com/blog/what-percentage-of-small-businesses-fail.*

Nassim Nicholas Taleb (TalebWisdom). "Actually Almost Everything I've Written That Has Survived Was Written When I Didn't Try to Get Anything Done." Twitter. April 22, 2020. *https://twitter.com/TalebWisdom/status/1252745298759372800?s=19.*

CHAPTER 8: THE CHANCE EFFECT (OR CAUSE AND EFFECT FALLACY)

Arthur, W. Brian. "Positive Feedbacks in the Economy." *Scientific American* 262, no. 2 (1990): 92–99. Accessed May 27, 2021. *http://www.jstor.org/stable/24996687.*

Encyclopedia Britannica Online. s.v. "David Hume." Accessed on September 18, 2021. *https://www.britannica.com/biography/David-Hume.*

Gladwell, Malcolm. *Blink: The Power of Thinking without Thinking.* New York City: Little, Brown and Co. 2005.

Statista. "The 100 Largest Companies in the World by Market Capitalization in 2020." Accessed May 27, 2021. *https://www.statista.com/statistics/263264/top-companies-in-the-world-by-market-capitalization/.*

Taleb, Nassim Nicholas. *Fooled by Randomness.* New York: Random House, 2nd Ed., 2005.

Trejos, Cristian, Adrian Van Deemen, Yeny E. Rodríguez, and Juan M. Gómez. "Overconfidence and Disposition Effect in the Stock Market: A Micro World Based Setting." *Journal of Behavioral and Experimental Finance*, Elsevier, Vol. 21(C) (2019): 61–69. *https://doi.org/10.1016/j.jbef.2018.11.001.*

Uppal, Jinny. "The Nature of Existence—Musings from Yoga Vasiṣṭha." *Blog* (blog) October 13, 2021. *https://www.jinnyuppal. com/blog/the-nature-of-existence-musings-from-yoga-vasiha.*

Venkatesananda, Swami. *The Concise Yoga Vasistha.* Albany, NY: State University of New York Press, 1985.

CHAPTER 9: THE POWER OF SILENCE

Bariso, Justin. "Intelligent Minds like Tim Cook and Jeff Bezos Embrace the Rule of Awkward Silence. You Should Too." *INC. COM*, September 9, 2020. *https://www.inc.com/justin-bariso/ intelligent-minds-like-tim-cook-jeff-bezos-embrace-rule-of-awkward-silence-you-should-too.html.*

Coppola, Francis F, dir. *The Godfather.* Hollywood, California: Paramount Pictures, 1972.

Curhan, Jared, Jennifer Overbeck, Yeri Cho, Teng Zhang and Yu Yang. "Silence Is Golden: Extended Silence, Deliberative Mindset, and Value Creation in Negotiation." *Researchgate* (November 2020). *https://www.researchgate.net/publica-tion/346503243_Silence_is_golden_Extended_silence_delib-erative_mindset_and_value_creation_in_negotiation.*

Goldminz, Itamar. "A Silent Meeting Is Worth a Thousand Words." *Medium* (blog). December 4, 2018. Accessed on May 27, 2021. *https://medium.com/org-hacking/a-silent-meeting-is-worth-a-thousand-words-ricau-henry-f6565b2ffb0a.*

Goodreads. "Margaret Atwood, Quotes, Quotable Quote." Accessed on September 12, 2021. *https://www.goodreads.com/ quotes/815563-if-you-can-t-say-anything-nice-don-t-say-any-thing-at.*

Jonathan Field. "Steve Jobs Insult Response." December 2, 2016. Video, 5:14. *https://www.youtube.com/watch?v=oeqPrUm-Vz-o&ab_channel=JonathanField.*

Locke, Taylor. "Jeff Bezos: This Is the 'Smartest Thing We Ever Did' at Amazon." *CNBC,* October 14, 2019. *https://www.cnbc. com/2019/10/14/jeff-bezos-this-is-the-smartest-thing-we-ever-did-at-amazon.html.*

Rogelberg, Steven G. And Liana Kreamer. "The Case for More Silence in Meetings." *Harvard Business Review,* June 14, 2019. *https://hbr.org/2019/06/the-case-for-more-silence-in-meetings.*

Samarin, William John. "Language of Silence." *Practical Anthropology,* 12:3 (1965): 115–119.

YouTube. "Iconic 'You're No Jack Kennedy' Debate Moment." October 3, 2016. Video, 4:04. *https://www.youtube.com/ watch?v=QYAZkczhdMs&ab_channel=CBSNews.*

CHAPTER 10: DAYDREAMING AND MIND-WANDERING AS CREATIVE TOOLS

Glausiusz, Josie. "Devoted to Distraction." *Psychology Today,* March 1, 2009. *https://www.psychologytoday.com/us/articles/200903/devoted-distraction.*

Goodreads. "Sukhraj S. Dhillon, Quotes." Accessed on September 12, 2021. *https://www.goodreads.com/author/quotes/3079725. Sukhraj_S_Dhillon.*

Raichle, Marcus E., Ann Mary Macleod and Abraham Z Snyder. "A Default Mode of Brain Function." *National Academy of Sciences*, 98(2) (2001): 676-682. *https://www.pnas.org/content/98/2/676.*

Suttie, Jill. "How Mind-Wandering May Be Good for You." *The Greater Good Magazine,* February 14, 2018. *https://greatergood.berkeley.edu/article/item/how_mind_wandering_may_be_good_for_you.*

Thich Nhat Hanh. *Being Peace.* Berkley, California: Parallax Press, 2005.

YouTube, "What Your Brain Does When You're Doing Nothing," January 9, 2019. Video, 5:55. *https://www.youtube.com/watch?v=0r15-Xde66s&list=PL3I0YRf9jc52O-7665Klk_pH-n4x-PIR6P&index=8&ab_channel=BrainFacts.org.*

Zedelius, Claire M. and Jonathan W. Schooler. "Mind-wandering 'Ahas' versus Mindful Reasoning: Alternative Routes to Creative Solutions." *Frontiers in Psychology*, Vol No. 6 (2015): 834. *https://doi.org/10.3389/fpsyg.2015.00834.*

CHAPTER 11: BEING LAZY AND PROCRASTINATING YOUR WAY TO RESULTS

Chun Chu, Angela Hsin and Choi Jin Nam. "Rethinking Procrastination: Positive Effects of 'Active' Procrastination Behavior on Attitudes and Performance." *The Journal of Social Psychology* 145, No. 3 (2005): 245-264. *https://doi.org/10.3200/SOCP.145.3.245-264.*

Goodreads. "Bill Gates, Quotes, Quotable Quote." Accessed on September 12, 2021. *https://www.goodreads.com/quotes/568877-i-choose-a-lazy-person-to-do-a-hard-job.*

Grant, Adam. *Originals: How Non-conformists Move the World.* New York: Viking, 2016.

Merriam Webster Online. s.v. "Hardworking." Accessed on September 12,2021. *https://www.merriam-webster.com/dictionary/ hardworking.*

Spielberg, Steven, dir. *Catch Me If You Can.* Universal City, CA: Amblin Entertainment and Parkes/MacDonald Productions, 2002.

Wikiquote. "Kurt Von Hammerstein-Equord." Accessed on September 12, 2021. *https://en.m.wikiquote.org/wiki/Kurt_von_ Hammerstein-Equord.*

CHAPTER 12: DECONSTRUCTING DICHOTOMIES

Bazerman, Max. "Dealmaking: Why It's Tempting to Trust Your Gut." *Program on Negotiation Harvard Law School Daily Blog* (blog). December 5, 2013. Accessed on May 28, 2021. *https:// www.pon.harvard.edu/daily/dealmaking-daily/dealmaking- why-its-tempting-to-trust-your-gut/.*

Duckworth, Angela. *Grit: The Power of Passion and Perseverance.* New York: Scribner/Simon & Schuster, 2016.

Gita, Bhagavad. "Bhagavad Gita: Chapter 4, Verse 18." Accessed on May 28, 2021. *https://www.holy-bhagavad-gita.org/chapter/4/ verse/18.*

Gladwell, Malcolm. *Blink: The Power of Thinking without Thinking.* New York: Little, Brown and Co., 2005.

Grant, Adam. *Think Again: The Power of Knowing What You Don't Know.* London: Penguin Publishing Group, 2021.

Radhakrishnan.S. *The Bhagavadgita.* India: Blackie & Son (India) Ltd., 1948.

Raichle, Marcus E., Ann Mary Macleod and Abraham Z Snyder. "A Default Mode of Brain Function." *National Academy of Sciences*, 98(2) (2001): 676-682. *https://www.pnas.org/content/98/2/676.*

Shankar, Shri Shri Ravi. *Ashtavakra Gita.* Sri Sri Publications Trust, 1st Edition, 2010.

Thorngate, W. "Possible Limits on a Science of Social Behavior." In *Social Psychology in Transition*, edited by Strickland L.h., Aboud F.e., Gergen K.j., 121-139. Boston: Springer, 1976. *https://doi.org/10.1007/978-1-4615-8765-1_9.*